Making Wooden
DINOSAURS

Making Wooden
DINOSAURS

Plans and Instructions with Notes on Each Species

RICHARD D. POUGHER

STACKPOLE
BOOKS

Published by
STACKPOLE BOOKS
5067 Ritter Road
Mechanicsburg, PA 17055

Printed in the United States of America

10 9 8 7 6 5 4 3 2 1

FIRST EDITION

Cover design by Wendy Reynolds
Cover drawing and photograph by Richard D. Pougher

Library of Congress Cataloging-in-Publication Data
Pougher, Richard D.
    Making wooden dinosaurs: plans and instructions with notes on each species / Richard D. Pougher.
      p. cm.
    Includes bibliographical references.
    ISBN 0-8117-2992-3
    1. Wooden toy making. 2. Mechanical toys. 3. Dinosaurs in art
  I. Title.
TT174.5.W6P68 1997   97-13866
745.592—dc21   CIP

To India Elspeth

Contents

Introduction

This book consists of thirteen sets of patterns and instructions that will enable the woodworker to create detailed, movable model dinosaurs for either toys or display. There are also three sets of patterns and directions for the construction of prehistoric plants, which will make for a more lifelike setting in which to show or play with the completed animals.

The dinosaurs chosen for the plans are representative of a variety of types and time periods. Each set of patterns was thoroughly researched and incorporates the latest concepts about how these creatures looked. Furthermore, all are to scale, with the result that, when finished, some models will be fairly large and others relatively small. It is hoped these designs will give the builder a good comparative sense of the incredible diversity of sizes and shapes of these animals.

Included with each set of plans is a brief, factual description of the dinosaur itself, in which its physical appearance and lifestyle are discussed. Because paleontological opinion seriously differs on many of these matters, the various scientific viewpoints and controversies surrounding each creature are also presented. While I opt for some of the newer, more radical theories (as will be apparent from the text and patterns), you are left to make up your own mind about these issues. For further reading, a select bibliography is included at the end of the book.

The plans are all full-scale unless otherwise noted, and each set is accompanied by detailed written instructions and photographs of the procedures. In terms of difficulty, the plans are organized from fairly simple to relatively complex. The first set of plans and instructions, those for Camptosaurus, includes all the basic construction methods applicable to the other dinosaurs. You are strongly encouraged to make this model first in order to become familiar with the required techniques, and then progress. Additional procedures needed to finish more advanced models are discussed in detail as necessary, and models requiring similar procedures are grouped together. All models require a fair amount of precision cutting and drilling. Certain aspects of a couple of the more advanced patterns are rather tricky. Still, they can be done, and done well, as the photographs of the completed models show. Remember, for the sake of both safety and producing a nice finished object, take your time. Good luck, and have fun!

General Construction

SAFETY CONSIDERATIONS

Safety, when using power tools, is the highest consideration. It is not the intent of this book to teach you how to use your band saw, router, or other tools. The reader is expected to have experience using the required woodworking tools. Be sure to read, understand, and follow the instructions that come with your tools, and when using any tool, wear safety glasses. Finally, be sure to read and understand the directions for making the dinosaur models before attempting to construct them.

Many of the patterns necessitate fairly close work with a router and, especially, a band saw. All parts can, however, be produced safely if you take your time. If you feel uncomfortable working very close with any given piece, cut as close as you can, and then remove additional stock via carving, sanding, or rasping. It may take a little longer, but your fingers are important. You know your capabilities and limits. Do not attempt any of these patterns while under the influence of alcohol. If you are so inclined, save that beer for the celebration of a job well done.

Precautions for Toy Dinosaurs

Of the utmost importance are two considerations that need be kept in mind if the finished product is to be used as a toy by children. The first, and most important, is that all spikes, horns, claws, and tips of tails should be suitably blunted. Second, all parts should be thoroughly sanded to avoid potential splinters. On the other hand, if you are an adult child, like myself, who enjoys playing, and the dinosaur is intended for personal use, the first of these considerations can be ignored. Still, you will want a nice finish, which involves thorough fine sanding.

WOODS

While the choice of woods is entirely up to you, it is recommended that common hardwoods such as oak, cherry, mahogany, or black walnut be employed. If the dinosaur is meant to be a toy, using a hardwood will produce a sturdier product with greater longevity. If it is intended for display, then a more aesthetically pleasing object will be had. Except for the trees and plants, pines are considered unacceptable. (For photographic reasons, however, most of the parts shown in the pictures are actually of lighter-colored softwoods.) Truly soft varieties, such as white, are too soft and not terribly pretty. Yellow pine, which is harder and more pleasing to the eye should not be used because of the extreme inconsistencies in the density of the grain. Much of the required drill work is quite precise and needs to be done without the aid of a drill press. Experiments with yellow pine for the dinosaurs have proven to be failures, because even with a brad-point type, the bit will walk or jump and chew up the stock. The bottom line in selecting wood is that even the largest dinosaur does not take much to make, and consequently, any additional cost for a better grade of material is minimal. If the finished dinosaur is strictly for show and the pocketbook allows it, then visually striking hardwoods like purple heart or zebra have great potential for a truly fine creation.

REQUIRED MATERIALS

Various woods (see specific patterns for required amounts)

$1/8$-, $3/16$-, $1/4$-, $3/8$-, and $1\frac{1}{4}$-inch dowel rods*

Round toothpicks

$1/4$- and $3/8$-inch commercial axle pegs or hardwood buttons or plugs (depending on type of leg construction)

A variety of rubber O-rings with $1/8$-, $3/16$-, $1/4$-, $5/16$- and $3/8$-inch openings, or an old inner tube

Oils, stains, varnishes, or paints

*Note: Only a short length of the last size is needed for a specific model. The $3/8$-inch-diameter dowel rod is necessary only if you opt for using the variation on Type A leg construction (see Camptosaurus).

REQUIRED TOOLS

Band saw with $3/16$-inch or $1/4$-inch blade
Router with the following bits:
    $1/4$-inch round-over
    $3/8$-inch round-over
    $3/8$-inch chamfer
    $3/4$-straighter rabbeting bit (optional if you
       have a 1-inch Forstner drill bit)
Router table
Electric hand drill with the following bits:*
    $3/64$-inch
    $1/16$-inch
    $3/32$-inch
    $1/8$-inch brad point
    $3/16$-inch brad point
    $1/4$-inch brad point
    $5/16$-inch brad point
    $3/8$-inch brad point
    $3/4$-inch brad point or Forstner
    1- or 2-inch Forstner (optional if you have
       a $3/4$-inch straight or rabbeting router bit)
Belt sander with medium- and fine-grit belts
Carving or modeling knife with razor edge
Table saw
Awl

Small, clear, flexible ruler
Small square
Small wood or modeling clamps that will
    encompass $3^1/2$ inches
Center finder for dowel rods
Wood glue
A lot of medium- and fine-grit sandpaper
Grade #0000 steel wool
    In addition, the following tools, which are not
absolutely necessary, will make life much easier:
    Planer
    Orbital sander
    Drill press or drill stand for electric hand drill
    Small, electric modeling tool (such as a Dremel)
       for fine work
    Set of rifflers
    Small diameter drum sander, or small, tapered
       grinding wheel for use on electric drill
    Small, fine-tooth hand saw such as a gents or
       dovetail
    Scroll saw for cutting smaller parts
    *Note: All the finished models shown were actually done using only a handheld power drill. For the sake of the photographs, a small drill press was used for holes requiring a 90-degree angle.

When selecting wood, strive for a dramatic grain that will enhance the appearance. Also consider using contrasting woods, for example, cherry for the legs and black walnut for the body. The employment of an additional wood does not mean that extra costs will be incurred. Frequently, the legs for one dinosaur can be cut from the scraps left over from the body of another. Many leg patterns, and even some of those for bodies, are ideal for using those nice, small pieces of scrap wood saved from previous projects. When cutting the legs for any given project, try to get all four out of the same piece of wood so there will be consistency in the final finish. For teeth, claws, and spikes, standard birch dowel rods or round toothpicks will be used to create the impression of bone or horn.

FINISHING

All of the photographed examples were treated with a glossy tung oil, which allows the natural beauty of the wood to be seen. This type of finish lends itself to

these models, as it is merely rubbed on with a soft cloth. It also works well because there are a lot of nooks and crannies that require treatment. For these areas, apply the tung oil with a small brush to ensure coverage, wipe off the excess, and rub in what remains. Of course, stains or varnishes can also be used, and stains are needed for the heads of axle pegs used to secure the legs.

These dinosaurs can be painted. If you choose to paint your dinosaurs, then the considerations about contrasting woods and dramatic grains are not important. There are, however, other important factors to keep in mind. We have no idea what colors dinosaurs really were. Undoubtedly, they were similar to those of animals today. Some were likely brightly hued or camouflaged, others quite drab. In any case, while coloring is left to the imagination, garish shades should be avoided in favor of more natural tones. Color schemes can range from solid shades overall, to mottled, to contrasting upper and lower body areas. Teeth, spikes, and claws should be

A table saw can be used to attain requisite thickness of stock. (The blade safety cover was removed only for the purpose of taking this photograph.)

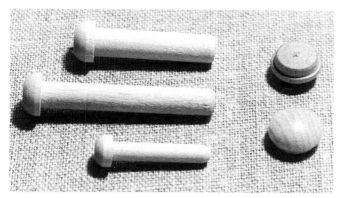

Commercial axle pegs and hardwood buttons (above) and O-rings (below) come in an assortment of sizes.

left off-white or ivory, eyes should be dark, and the insides of mouths should be red or dark pink.

ATTAINING REQUISITE THICKNESS OF STOCK

While many of the parts are to be fashioned from standard 1-inch dimensional stock ($^3/4$-inch actual thickness), many are to be made from materials of $^1/4$- to $^5/8$-inch stock (actual thickness). If you do not have a planer (few of us do), the following procedure will produce the desired results if you own or have access to a table saw. Because none of these thinner pieces are very wide, the fence in association with the blade height can simply be set on a table saw, and the stock sliced to the desired thickness. This should, however, be done only if the length of the section of wood is sufficient to exceed by a considerable margin the total diameter of the saw blade. For safety reasons, always use a push stick when passing the wood through the saw. After cutting, sand out any irregularities created during the process.

AXLE PEGS AND DOWEL RODS

All models require the use of commercial axle pegs and dowel rods. Frequently, however, these are not the exact size they are said to be. For instance, a $^1/4$-inch axle peg might actually be only $^3/16$ inch in diameter. Therefore, because a snug fit is desired, when drilling holes, select a bit equal in size to the real diameter of the axle peg or dowel rod. In essence, although the instructions may call for a hole for a $^1/4$-inch axle peg, a $^3/16$-inch drill bit might actually be more appropriate.

Also, with axle pegs, the diameter of the head is as important as that of the peg proper. Except for large legs, the heads of $^1/4$-inch and $^3/8$-inch pegs should not exceed $^3/8$ inch and $^1/2$ inch, respectively.

Scientific Facts and Theories on Dinosaurs

The Age of Dinosaurs began 225 million years ago and lasted for 160 million years. The time period in which they lived was the Mesozoic, which is divided into three periods, the Triassic, Jurassic, and Cretaceous. The first true dinosaurs, such as Plateosaurus, came into existence during the Upper or Late Triassic. The Jurassic period followed and was the time of Apatosaurs, Allosaurs, Stegosaurs, Camptosaurs, and Ceratosaurs. The Cretaceous period, which lasted until 65 million years ago, was populated with Tyrannosaurs, Ceratopsians, Hadrosaurs, Ornithomimids, and Pachycephalosaurs. Dinosaurs, considered the most successful group of animals to have existed because of the length of time they were on earth, ranged in size from the chicken-sized Compsognathus to the mighty Supersaurus, estimated to stand over 50 feet tall, and the Ultrasaurus, even larger.

In recent years, dinosaurs have undergone a considerable amount of scientific reexamination, resulting in a number of significant new theories. One of the most important new concepts is that dinosaurs were not cold-blooded, reptilian creatures. Instead, many authorities now maintain they were warm-blooded like modern mammals and birds. The new theories have led to much serious debate among paleontologists.

Traditionally, dinosaurs have been viewed as slow-moving, dull-witted beasts with cold-blooded, or ectothermic, metabolisms like modern snakes, lizards, and alligators. With such a metabolism, an animal cannot regulate its own body heat. It must rely on an external source, the sun, for warmth that can be processed into energy. It was believed that because many dinosaurs were so big, requiring an incredible amount of warmth to produce energy, they could be nothing other than slow, ponderous beasts.

Then, the new and radical theory that dinosaurs were warm-blooded emerged. Warm-blooded, or endothermic, animals such as mammals and birds attain their energy through food. Thus they can regulate their own body temperature and are not reliant on external sources for energy. As such, they can sustain a much higher level of activity over longer periods of time, day or night. Proponents of warm-

MESOZOIC TIME LINE

Plateosaurus

Lower	TRIASSIC	Upper
225 million years		190 million years

bloodedness support their ideas with substantial evidence.

One group of arguments upholding that dinosaurs were endotherms relates to their physical structure. Size is a consideration with these scientists. They believe that large dinosaurs, if ectotherms, could not possibly absorb enough sunlight during the course of a day to produce enough energy to move much, if at all. Consequently, large predators could not possibly hunt, chase, and attack prey.

In conjunction, the structure of dinosaur legs is more like that of warm-blooded mammals than of cold-blooded reptiles. Basically, dinosaur legs were straight and positioned directly beneath the body. They had a truly erect stance. The legs of reptiles are bent with the upper portion projecting out to the sides. Also, the general physical makeup of dinosaurs, especially bipedal carnivorous theropods, indicates that many were built for speed and agility, which would be impossible with a cold-blooded metabolism. The length ratio of upper to lower leg bones of many dinosaurs further supports that they were capable of rapid movement. And sustained speed and agility require a high metabolic rate.

Relative to these arguments is the fact that the teeth of both herbivorous and carnivorous dinosaurs indicate that they ate a great deal of food, which further supports their being warm-blooded.

An examination of the composition of fossilized dinosaur bones adds much weight to the theory of their being endothermic. In essence, the arrangement and number of blood vessels are similar to that of mammals and birds rather than reptiles. This also indicates a rapid growth rate indicative of warm-blooded animals.

The behavior patterns of dinosaurs also point to their being warm-blooded as well. Many types lived in herds, and at least some actively cared for their young. The proportion of carnivores to herbivores in the fossil record is also used as an argument. The low ratio of predators to prey is like that of mammals. This is indicative of an ecosystem in which a large food supply is needed to maintain predators with a high metabolic rate. With reptilian predators, which do not require as much food, the ratio is much higher.

In defense, those scientists still favoring cold-bloodedness pose a number of counterarguments. The most prevalent is that if the larger dinosaurs were warm-blooded, they simply could not eat enough food to maintain their metabolism. They also believe that dinosaur legs, despite their positioning and bone ratios, were not strong enough for rapid movement with the larger species. Basically, speed would create too much shock and stress, causing the bones to fracture. Finally, some dinosaurs had fins and plates, which are often interpreted as cooling systems. Such would only be necessary if the animals were cold-blooded.

While the above ideas reflect the concepts of two opposing lines of thought, a third group, more moderate in its concepts, has emerged. These scientists uphold that at least the large dinosaurs were cold-blooded, but they maintained their energy levels

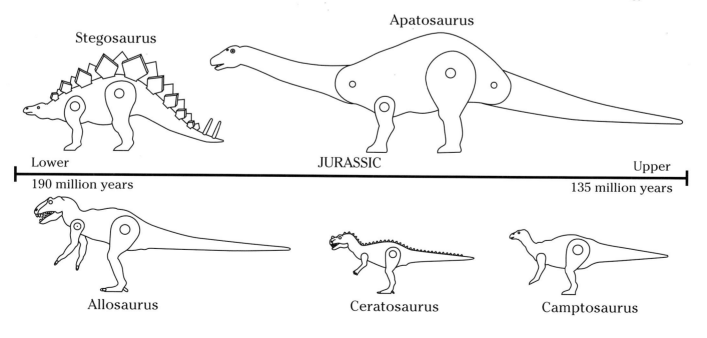

Stegosaurus

Apatosaurus

Lower   JURASSIC   Upper

190 million years   135 million years

Allosaurus   Ceratosaurus   Camptosaurus

through a process called homeothermy. This relies on the idea that the larger the animal, the less external surface area there is relative to its mass. Consequently, it was able to maintain absorbed heat because it gave off relatively little. In turn, the creature was little affected by changes in temperature, and it needed to rely on external energy sources much less.

The supporters of the warm-blooded theory counter that most dinosaurs were small to midsized, and thus their surface-to-volume ratio was increased. In response, some primarily traditional theorists admit that perhaps some of the smaller lines of dinosaurs were in fact warm-blooded, while maintaining that the larger ones were cold-blooded.

Perhaps the most serious argument for warm-bloodedness arises from another serious new concept: that an evolutionary branch of one line of dinosaurs, the Coelurosaurs, ultimately evolved into modern birds, which are endotherms. It is maintained that at least some dinosaurs had feathers, which further advances the argument for their evolving into birds and being warm-blooded. Feathers, like fur, are an insulator required by warm-blooded creatures.

All of this debate has led to efforts by some to reclassify dinosaur taxonomy. Traditionally, they are grouped in the subclass Archosauria in the class Reptilia. In turn, the true dinosaurs are divided into two orders, Saurischia, "lizard-hipped," and Ornithischia, "bird-hipped." The first order, Saurischia, was further divided into the suborders Theropoda, which included Allosaurus, Tyrannosaurus, Ceratosaurus, and Ornithomimus; and Sauropoda, which included Apatosaurus (Brontosaurus), Diplodocus, and the Prosauropod Plateosaurus. The second order, Ornithischia, was composed of the Camptosaurs; the Hadrosaurs, such as Lambeosaurus and Corythosaurus; the Ceratopsians, including Monoclonius and Styracosaurus; the Stegosaurs; and the Ankylosaurs.

Now this traditional ordering is being challenged in light of the new theories. Most significantly, many paleontologists have removed dinosaurs from the class Reptilia and assigned them their own class, Archosauria. Dinosauria is now a subclass or infraclass of this group. Some even wish to assign dinosaurs to the class of birds, or vice versa. Within these large classifications, there has been considerable rearrangement of species, genus, and families between taxonomic levels. A number of the new classifications are outlined in the discussions of the specific dinosaurs that follow.

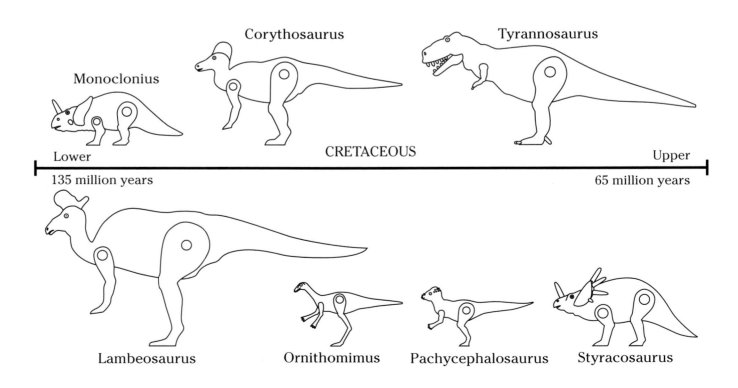

DINOSAUR PROJECTS

Camptosaurus: Making the Basic Dinosaur

Camptosaurus (KAMP-tuh-sawr-us): "Bent lizard"
Order: Ornithischia, "bird hipped"
Suborder: Ornithopoda, "bird footed"
Family: Camptosauridae
Genus: *Camptosaurus*

Close relatives: Callovosaurus and Honghesaurus
Length: Up to 23 feet (7 meters). Small, turkey-sized versions are known, but these probably represent young animals rather than a separate species
Height: About 7 feet (2 meters) at the hip
Weight: Perhaps as much as 2,000 pounds (907.2 kilograms)

Camptosaurus lived in what is now western Europe and the western United States. Its fossilized skeletons are found in the Upper (Late) Jurassic Kimmeridge Clay of Oxfordshire, England, and the Morrison Formation of Wyoming. A major evolutionary success, these docile planteaters probably survived into the Cretaceous period.

Camptosaurus's rather bulky body was primarily supported by its powerful hind legs. On the back feet, hooflike claws appeared on the first four of the five toes. The forelimbs were only about half the length of the rear, but were themselves sturdy appendages. The same hooflike claws existed on the fingers, but only on the first three of the five. Their presence indicates the hands were used for walking rather than grasping, despite the shorter length of the front limbs. Given the difference in size between the front and back, it is evident that Camptosaurus was capable of movement on either two or four legs. In essence, carrying its stiffened tail off the ground to act as a counterbalance for the front portion of the body, this animal undoubtedly normally walked from place to place on just its rear legs but dropped to all four when leisurely browsing for low-growing plants. In fact, this ability to bend down to feed is what inspired its name, which means "bent lizard."

For eating, Camptosaurus had batteries of closely packed, chisel-shaped teeth along the sides of its mouth and a sharp, toothless beak in front. It has been suggested that in association, there may have

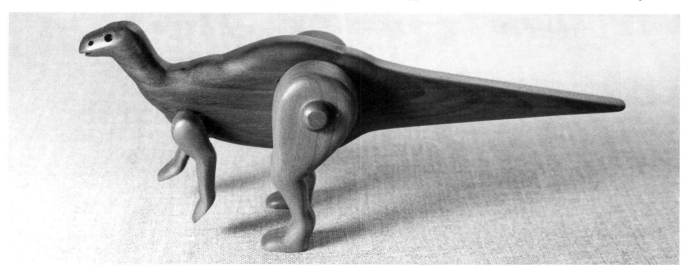

been a long, grasping tongue similar to a giraffe's. Quite possibly, Camptosaurus grabbed a plant with its tongue to pull it into its mouth, clipped it off with its beak, and chewed it with its teeth. The nature of the teeth indicates that the vegetation eaten was coarse and hard.

Next to the Sauropods, Camptosaurs were probably the most common animal of their time period. In the dinosaur world, they held a spot in the ecosystem similar to that of deer today. Their habitat consisted of open floodplain, which they shared with the Stegosaurs. Camptosaurs did not live in swamps or forests. It is likely they formed herds, and it was this social structure, offering safety in numbers, combined with their ability to run fast on their powerful hind legs, that constituted their only means of defense from such predators as Allosaurus and Ceratosaurus.

REQUIRED MATERIALS

Body: One $8^{1}/_{2}$ x 2 x $^{3}/_{4}$-inch piece of stock
Rear legs: Two $8^{1}/_{2}$ x $1^{3}/_{4}$ x $^{3}/_{4}$-inch pieces of stock*
Front legs: Two $7^{1}/_{2}$ x 1 x $^{1}/_{2}$-inch pieces of stock *
Other: Two $^{3}/_{8}$-inch-diameter axle pegs for rear legs and one $1^{1}/_{4}$-inch length of $^{3}/_{16}$-inch-diameter dowel rod for the arms
*Note: All arm and leg dimensions include additional wood required to leave an extension off the bottom of each foot. (See the section below on basic arm and leg construction.)

BODY CONSTRUCTION

The instructions for the Camptosaurus body incorporate all the basic procedures required to make the bodies, arms, and legs of the remaining dinosaurs. Consequently, to become familiar with the necessary techniques, you should construct the Camptosaurus first, before progressing. The increasingly more advanced models following Camptosaurus generally call for different sizes of drill and router bits, and require some additional or variant procedures. Such information is presented with each specific set of plans and instructions relative to those for Camptosaurus. All drawings are full-scale unless otherwise noted.

Step 1.
Lay out the body pattern (see fig. C2), keeping in mind that with this and all other models, the wood grain should run lengthwise with the body pattern. With an awl, mark the center points of the holes to be drilled for the arms and legs, and also the one eye and nostril on this side.

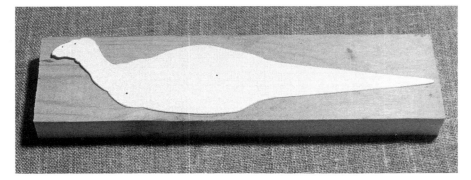

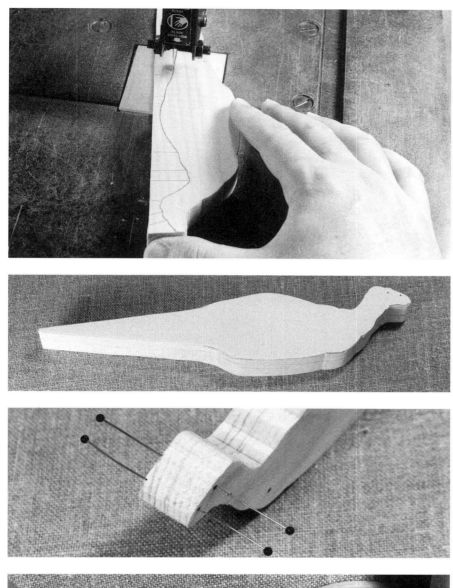

Step 2.
Using a band saw with a $^3/_{16}$- or $^1/_4$-inch blade, cut out the body. Either of these blade sizes is suitable for any band saw work required for the models.

Step 3.
After cutting, reverse the pattern to the opposite side and mark the holes for the other eye and nostril.

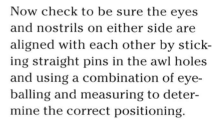

Now check to be sure the eyes and nostrils on either side are aligned with each other by sticking straight pins in the awl holes and using a combination of eyeballing and measuring to determine the correct positioning.

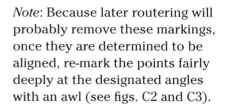

Note: Because later routering will probably remove these markings, once they are determined to be aligned, re-mark the points fairly deeply at the designated angles with an awl (see figs. C2 and C3).

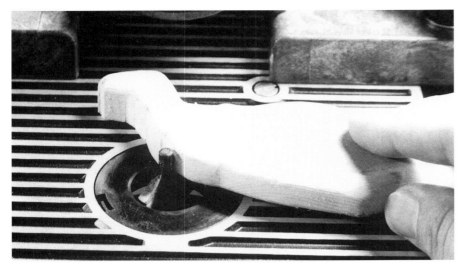

Step 4.

Using a $^3/_8$-inch round-over bit, router all around both sides of the body. For safety reasons, because this and other body pieces are relatively small and lightweight, do not attempt to cut to the full depth of the router bit in one pass. Make several passes (at least three), with the bit set to cut progressively deeper each time, and take the wood down gradually.

The router bit safety cover has been removed for this and all other photographs showing router use.

Step 5.

Drill the rear leg hole through the body to accommodate the axle pegs, using a $^3/_8$-inch or appropriate size brad-point bit (select the drill bit size according to the actual diameter of the axle peg). This and all other holes drilled in model bodies for arm and leg axle pegs should be executed at an angle of 90 degrees to the side of the body piece and should pass completely through the wood. Use a drill press or stand, if you have access to one, for all right-angle holes.

Step 6.

With a $^3/_{16}$-inch (or appropriate size) brad-point bit, drill the forward hole through the body in the same manner as above to accommodate the dowel rod for the front legs.

Step 7.
With a $1/8$-inch brad-point bit, at the center point of the round and at a 45-degree angle with the side of the body, drill the eye holes to a depth of $1/16$ inch (see fig. C3).

Step 8.
With a $1/16$-inch bit, at the center point of the round and at a 45-degree angle with the side of the body, drill the nostril holes to a depth of $1/16$ inch (see fig. C3).

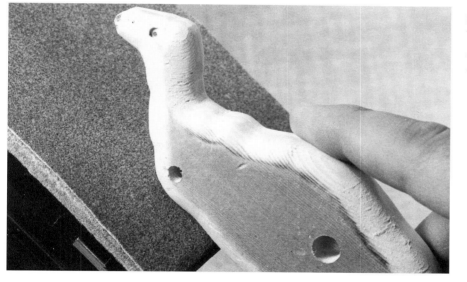

Step 9.
With medium-grit paper, sand out any irregularities in the body caused by cutting and routering.

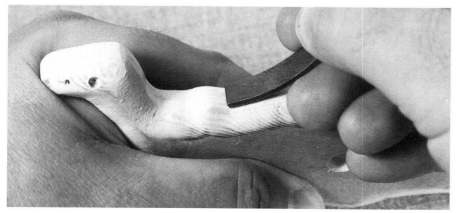

Although not necessary, if you have a small drum sander, a small tapered grinding wheel, or a set of rifflers, use them to clean up the angles and concave undulations on the body and other pieces. They will help save time and effort.

CARVING THE MOUTHS: TYPE A MOUTH

Most of the dinosaurs require a small amount of carving, involving the simplest of techniques, to create their mouths. The only essential tool is a small carving or modeling knife with a razor-sharp, curved blade.

Carving the Camptosaurus mouth (Type A mouth) involves two series of very simple cuts that combine in cross section to form a V-like groove (see fig. C4). The same procedure is used to create the mouths of the Corythosaurus, Lambeosaurus, Monoclonius and Styracosaurus.

Step 1.
Transfer the lines of the mouth from the pattern to the already cut and routered body piece. Draw these on both sides with a well-sharpened pencil, keeping them properly positioned and of equal dimensions on each side.

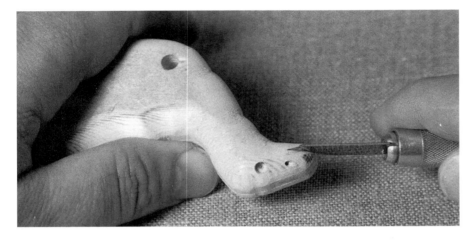

Step 2.
Along the upper line of the mouth, make a series of connected 90-degree cuts all around. Except toward the corners of the mouth, these should be about $1/16$ inch deep. As you near the corners, cut progressively shallower until the depth is virtually nothing at the corners themselves.

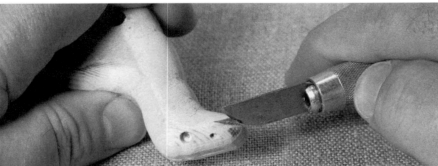

Step 3.
Along the lower line of the mouth, make a series of connected upward cuts all around at an angle of roughly 45 degrees (see fig. C4) that will meet at the designated depth with the first series. The undesired wood can then be simply lifted out.

Step 4.
If necessary, repeat these two steps in sequence.
Step 5.
With the knife or rifflers, even out any irregularities.

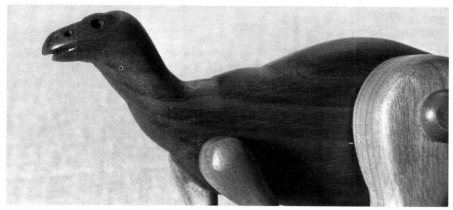

Completed Type A Mouth

Step 6.
Sand the areas from which the wood has been removed.

FINISHING
Step 1.
Fine-sand the body.
Step 2.
Finish as desired.

BASIC ARM AND LEG CONSTRUCTION

All dinosaur patterns employ one or, as with the Camptosaurus, both of the following procedures for arm and/or leg construction. The basic steps are described here, illustrated by the Camptosaurus, and you need to become familiar with them before progressing. Specific dimensions and tool sizes will vary with each set of dinosaur instructions, and some models require additional procedures.

Type A Arm and Leg Construction

Camptosaurus's rear legs are fashioned using this construction method (see figs. C5 and C6). It employs commercial axle pegs and is designed to allow independent movement of the arms and legs on a completed dinosaur. Both ¼- and ⅜-inch-diameter axle pegs are required to produce the various models. These can be purchased from most woodworker supply houses and hobby shops. Also needed are a variety of rubber O-rings or one old inner tube. For the sake of convenience and clarity, only legs and feet will be referred to in the following directions, but the same methods apply to arms and hands requiring this form of construction.

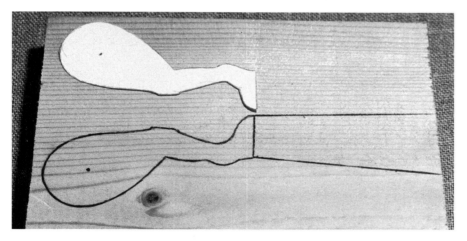

Layout, Cutting, and Drilling
Step 1.
Lay out the Camptosaurus rear leg pattern (see fig. C5), on the desired piece of wood keeping in mind that with this and all other leg patterns, the wood grain should run lengthwise with the pattern. Try to get all the legs for a dinosaur out of the same piece of wood so that there will be consistency in grain and color. When laying out a pair of legs, reverse the pattern for one so that there will be a corresponding right and left. Allow enough stock to leave at least a 4-inch extension off the bottom of each foot. This will give you something to hold on to when routering later. For smaller legs, increase the length of the extension accordingly.

Use a pencil to mark the lines for the bottom of the feet. With an awl, on what will be the outer face of the leg, mark the center point for the hole that will be drilled for the axle peg.

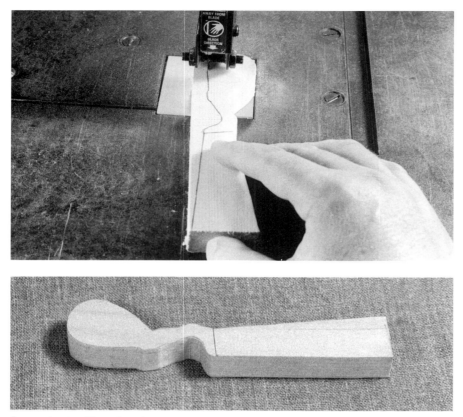

Step 2.
Using a band saw with a $^3/_{16}$- or $^1/_4$-inch blade, cut out each leg, being sure to leave the extension at the bottom of each foot.

Leg cutout with extension

Step 3.
With a $^3/_8$-inch round-over bit, using the extension on the foot bottom as a handle, completely router the edge of the leg and foot that will face out when finished. Keep your fingers well away from the router blade. Because many legs are relatively small, delicate, and lightweight, do not attempt to cut the full depth in one pass. Make several passes (at least three), with the bit set to cut progressively deeper each time, and take the wood down gradually. With each cut, router both legs in the pair so that they will be uniform. This step should be done in conjunction with the next step. The result will be a uniformity of cut all around and between each leg.

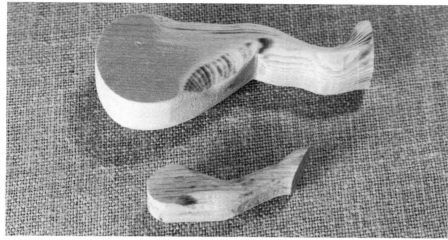

Step 4.
Using the same bit on what will be the back or inner side of the leg, router only the areas indicated. Basically, with all legs, the upper part of the inside of the leg should not be routered.

Inside of both front and rear legs routered

Step 5.
From what will be the outside of the leg, at the point designated in Step 1, drill the hole for the axle peg completely through the leg, using the same diameter brad-point drill bit as that used for the corresponding hole in the body. This and all other holes drilled through leg pieces for axle pegs should be executed at an angle of 90 degrees with the side of the leg.

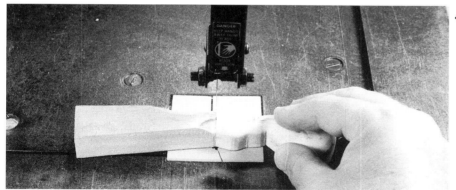

◀ **Step 6.**
Now use a band saw to cut the extension off each foot at the point indicated. Be sure that each leg in the pair is cut to exactly the same length, and that the angles of the cuts match.

Step 7.
With medium-grit paper, sand out any rough spots or irregularities created during cutting and routering.

Step 8.
Cut the two axle pegs to the appropriate length. Exclusive of the head, the length in all cases should equal the thickness of the leg plus one-half the thickness of the body (see fig. C7). For the Camptosaurus, the length will be 1⅛ inches plus the thickness of the head.

Step 9.
This step is for those dinosaurs, such as the Camptosaurus, meant to stand on their hind feet. With these, it is not intended that the tail touch whatever surface the dinosaur is standing on and act as a prop. To ensure this, proceed as follows. With the body completely assembled and the forelegs finished to this point as well, fit both pairs of legs to the body (without glue) and test the dinosaur on a flat surface. If it balances, proceed to Step 10. If it tips forward or backward, correct as follows (see fig. C6).

If the *dinosaur tips backward*, trim the bottoms of the feet at an angle, taking off only the smallest amount at a time. Begin at the point of the heel and progress to a slightly greater depth toward the toe. This will cause the weight of

the dinosaur to be thrown forward. Either cutting or sanding will accomplish the desired effect. Be sure to keep the bottoms of the feet perfectly flat, maintaining equivalent angles and legs of equal length. After each cut, reassemble the dinosaur and check for stability. Keep trimming and reassembling until balance is achieved.

If the *dinosaur tips forward*, (this should not be a problem) follow the same procedures as above, but reverse the angle of the cut from the toe to the heel. This will throw the weight backward and achieve balance.

Step 10.
At this point in the instructions for the other dinosaur models, any additional procedures needed to produce Type A legs will be discussed.

Finishing
Step 1.
Fine-sand legs and heads of axle pegs.
Step 2.
Treat legs with desired finish.
Step 3.
Stain or paint heads of axle pegs to match the finish on the legs. Do not finish the actual peg portion.

Assembly
Step 1.
If you are not using O-rings, cut washers from an old inner tube to a size large enough to fit over the axle peg but small enough not to be visible around the edge of the leg when assembled. These need not be fancy. The purpose of the O-ring or washer is to create friction between the leg and the body so the finished dinosaur will maintain whatever position it is posed in. Because of their diameter, thickness, and hardness, commercial washers are not recommended.

◄ Step 2.
With the leg completely finished, pass the axle peg through it, and place the O-ring or washer over the peg (see fig. C7).

Step 3.
With the body completely finished, use a toothpick to place some glue inside the hole in the body that will receive the axle peg. Be careful not to get any glue outside the hole on the surface that will be in contact with the leg.

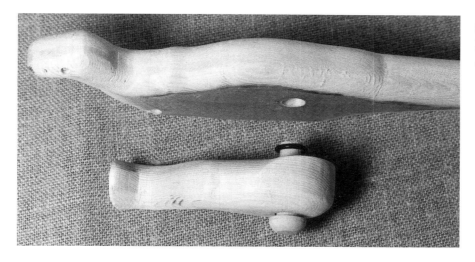

Step 4.
Insert the pegs for both the right and left legs at the same time.

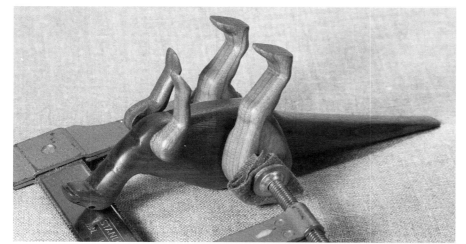

Step 5.
Pad the heads of the axle pegs, clamp under moderate pressure, and let the glue set.

Type A Leg Construction Variation

Based on the same concept and following the same basic procedures just outlined, this alternative form of construction can be used if you want a more aesthetically pleasing finished product for display purposes. This method involves making the axle pegs from dowel rods and commercial hardwood buttons or plugs of the same wood used for the legs (see fig. C7). Consequently, several additional steps are required and need be incorporated into the previous instructions prior to drilling the leg (Step 5).

Step 1.
Cut a dowel rod of the designated diameter to a length equal to the thickness of the leg plus one-half the thickness of the body. For Camptosaurus, the $3/16$-inch-diameter dowel should be $1\frac{1}{8}$ inches long.

◀ **Step 2.**
Find and mark the center point on the back of the button, and drill a hole equal to the diameter of the dowel rod halfway through.

Step 3.
Glue the button onto the dowel, making sure to keep it at a 90-degree angle.

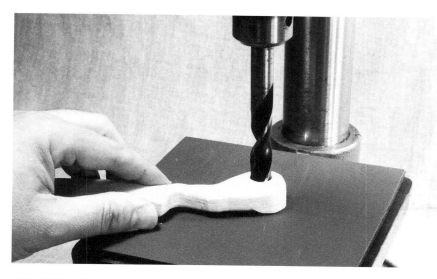

Step 4.
This method requires the hole through the leg to be countersunk in order to accommodate the button (see fig. C7). To an appropriate shallow depth, at the point indicated in Step 1, drill a hole large enough to receive the back of the button snugly. Do not drill all the way through the leg.

Then, at the center point of the first hole, drill a second, smaller one, equal to the diameter of the dowel, completely through the leg.

Step 5.
Proceed with Step 6 of basic Type A leg construction above.

Type B Arm and Leg Construction
The Camptosaurus's front legs require Type B construction (see figs. C5, C8, C9). This method is intended for arms or legs too small for axle pegs. Here, a single length of dowel rod is used rather than two axle pegs, and a pair will not move independently of each other. Again, although these directions are to be applied to arms and hands as well, only legs and feet are referred to in this section. The basic steps are the same as with the Type A method except as noted.

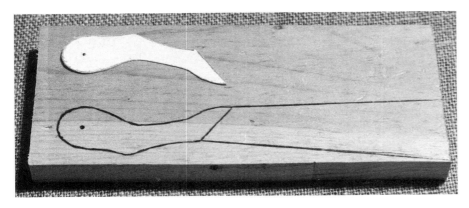

Layout, Cutting, and Drilling
Step 1.
Lay out the front legs using the same methods described for Type A, but mark the holes to be drilled for the dowel on what will be the inside of the legs. Although the Camptosaurus's front legs can be routered, some patterns requiring Type B construction are entirely too small to use this tool. In this case, it is not necessary to leave an extension off the bottom of the foot.

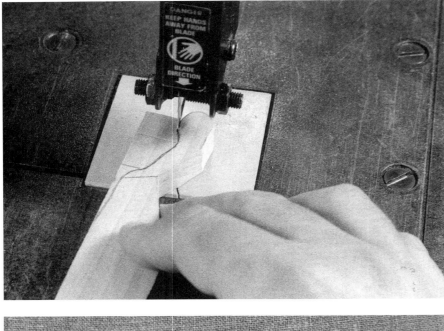

Step 2.
With the band saw, cut out the legs using the same procedures as for the Type A legs.

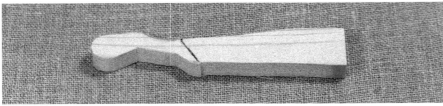

Leg cutout with extension

Step 3.
If you choose to router the front legs, do so at the designated points using a ¼-inch round-over bit, following the same procedures described for Type A legs.

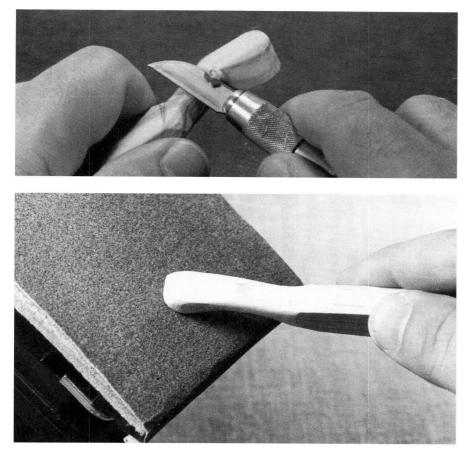

Step 4.
If the legs are not to be routered, then, except at the bottoms of the feet, merely break or soften the edge all around the outer face, and at the designated points on the inner, by carving or sanding.

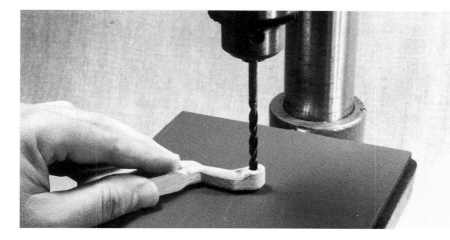

Step 5.
At the point indicated on the back side of the leg, drill a hole $\frac{1}{4}$ inch deep to accommodate the dowel rod, using a $\frac{3}{16}$-inch or appropriate size brad-point bit. (The drill bit should be the same size as that used to drill the matching hole through the body.) The depth of the hole drilled in any Type B leg should be half the thickness of the leg.

Step 6.
With the band saw, cut the extension off each leg at the point indicated.

◀ **Step 7.**
Cut the appropriate size dowel rod to a length equal to the thickness of the dinosaur's body plus the total of the depths of the holes in each leg. For Camptosaurus, the $3/16$-inch-diameter dowel should be $1^1/4$ inches long.

Finishing
Step 1.
Fine-sand the legs.
Step 2.
Treat legs with desired finish.

Assembly
Step 1.
With all parts completely finished, pass the dowel rod through the hole in the body so that it extends the same distance on either side (see fig. C8).

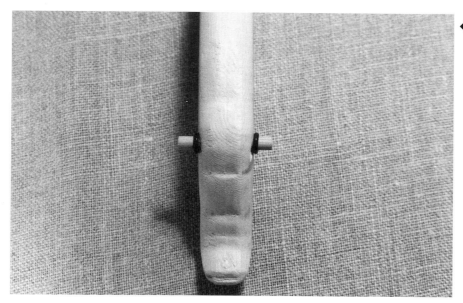

Step 2.
Place O-rings or washers cut to the appropriate size over the exposed ends of the dowel rod.

Step 3.
Use a toothpick to place a small amount of glue inside the hole in each leg. Be careful not to get any glue on the surface that will be in contact with the body.

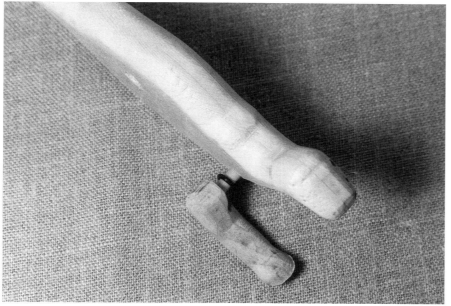

Step 4.
Place each leg over a dowel rod end. Because the legs in a pair will not move independently of each other, for those dinosaurs that stand on their hind legs and require Type B front legs, you may wish to glue them out of alignment (see fig. C9). This will create a more natural pose and give the effect of movement. For dinosaurs that stand on all fours, it is better to align the legs.

Step 5.
Pad the upper arm areas, clamp under moderate pressure, and let dry.

Congratulations! You just completed your first dinosaur.

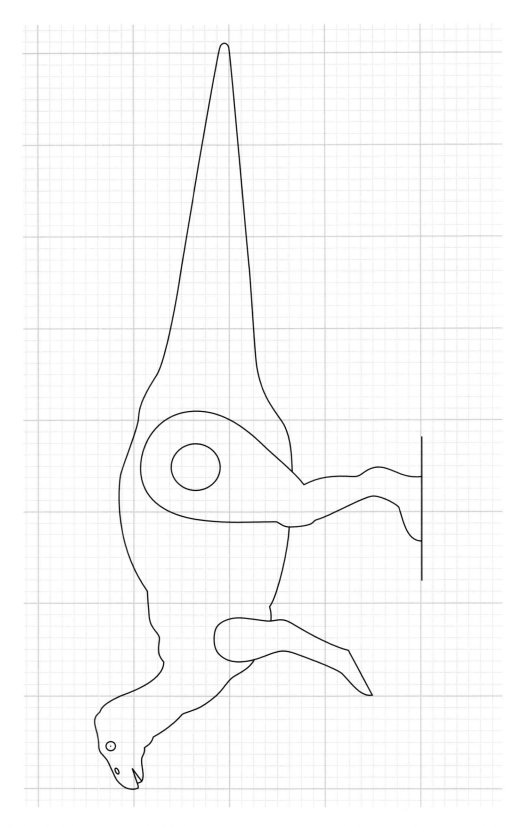

FIGURE C1. PLAN OF COMPLETED CAMPTOSAURUS (FULL-SCALE)

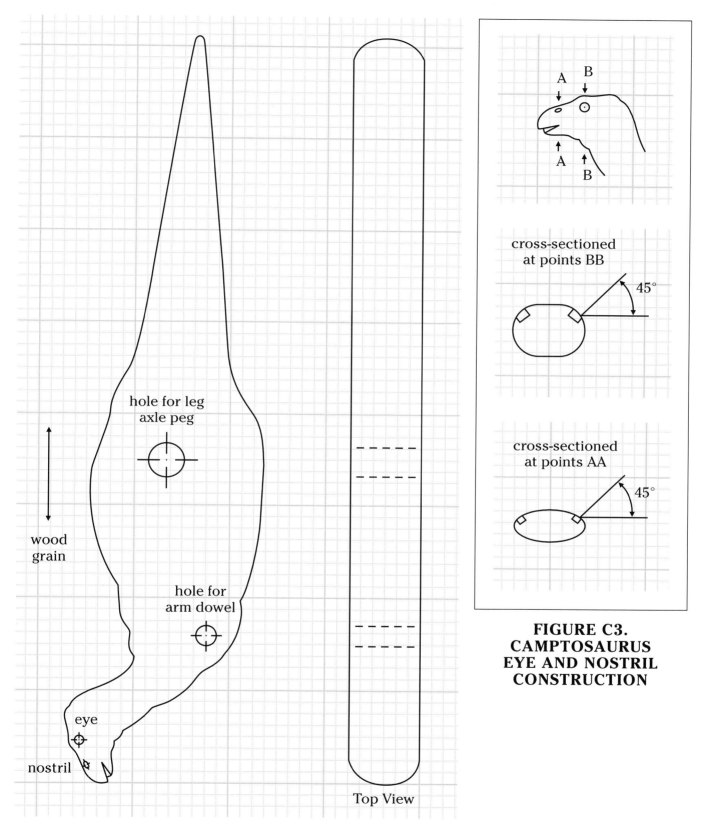

hole for leg
axle peg

wood
grain

hole for
arm dowel

eye

nostril

Top View

A

B

A

B

cross-sectioned
at points BB

45°

cross-sectioned
at points AA

45°

**FIGURE C3.
CAMPTOSAURUS
EYE AND NOSTRIL
CONSTRUCTION**

FIGURE C2. BODY PATTERN FOR CAMPTOSAURUS

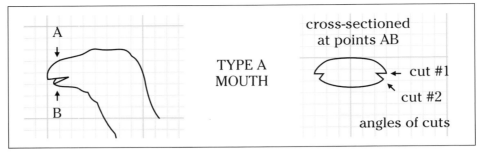

FIGURE C4.
CARVING THE CAMPTOSAURUS MOUTH

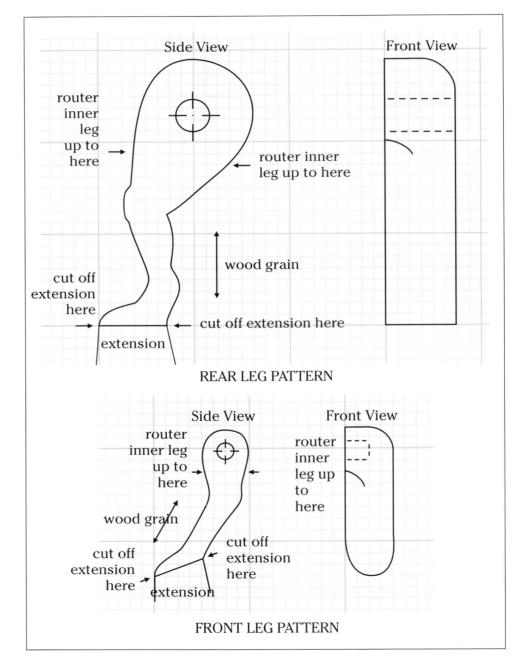

FIGURE C5. CAMPTOSAURUS LEG PATTERNS

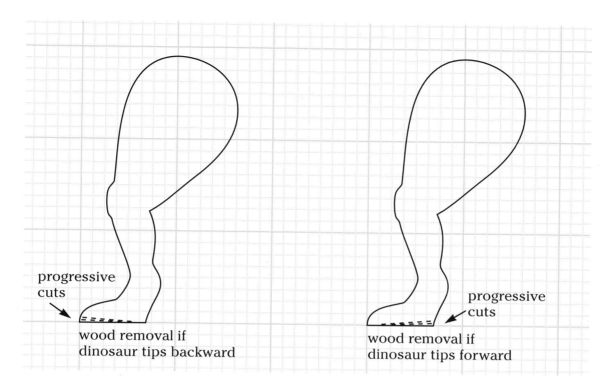

FIGURE C6.
GETTING A MODEL TO BALANCE ON TWO FEET

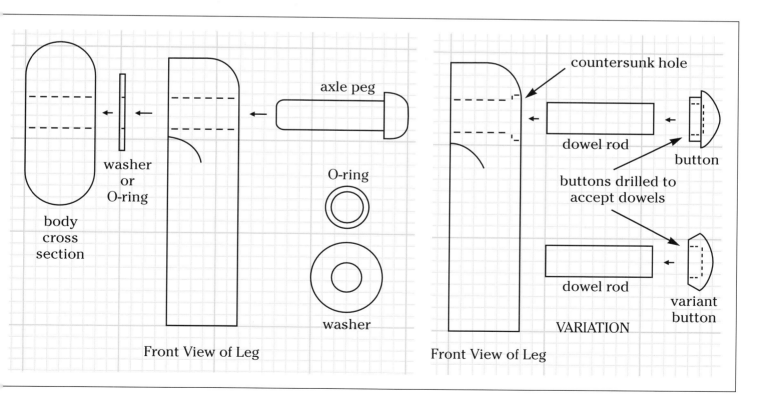

FIGURE C7. TYPE A LEG CONSTRUCTION AND VARIATION

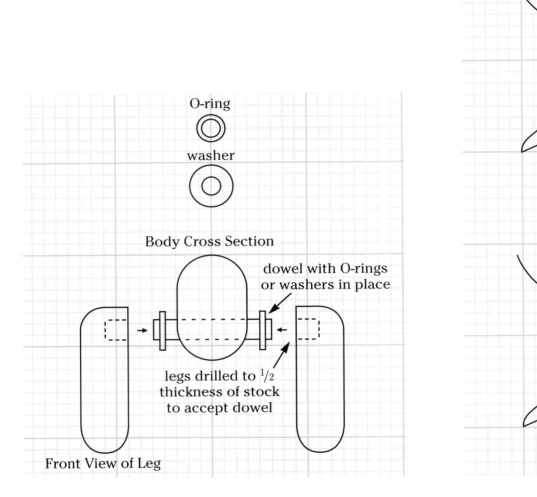

O-ring

washer

Body Cross Section

dowel with O-rings
or washers in place

legs drilled to $^1/_2$
thickness of stock
to accept dowel

Front View of Leg

aligned

unaligned

FIGURE C8. TYPE B LEG CONSTRUCTION

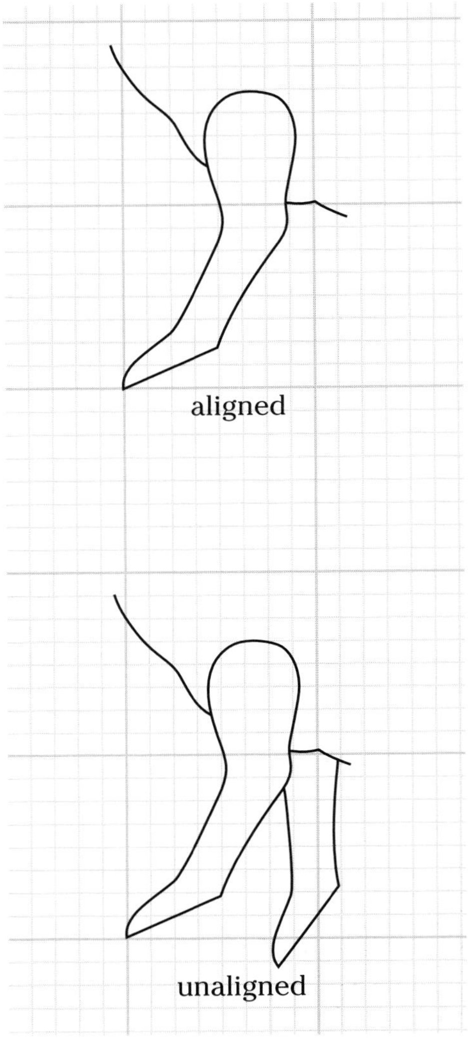

**FIGURE C9. ALIGNMENT
OF TYPE B LEGS**

Lambeosaurus lambei

Lambeosaurus (LAM-be-uh-sawr-us): "Lambe's lizard"
Order: Ornithischia, "bird-hipped"
Suborder: Ornithopoda, "bird-footed"
Family: Hadrosauridae
Subfamily: Lambeosaurine
Genus: *Lambeosaurus*
Species: *Lambeosaurus lambei*

Close relatives: Corythosaurus, Parasaurolophus, Hypacrosaurus, and Tsintaosaurus
Length: Perhaps up to 49 feet (14.94 meters)
Height: Perhaps up to 20 feet (6.096 meters) at the hip
Weight: Up to 3 tons (2.72 metric tons)

The first fossilized skeleton of a Lambeosaurus was uncovered in 1913 by Charles Sternberg in the Upper Cretaceous Oldman (Belly River) Formation at Red Deer River, Alberta, Canada. It was a significant find, because it was the first discovery of a crested Hadrosaur. Originally called Stephanosaurus, the animal was later renamed after Lawrence Lambe of the Canadian Geological Survey. Since then, additional Lambeosaurus remains have been found in Baja California.

Hadrosaurs, the family of so-called duck-billed dinosaurs because of the shape of their noses and mouths, were represented by two subfamilies: Hadrosaurines and Lambeosaurines. Lambeosaurus was a member of the latter group. All probably evolved in what is now Asia from a common Iguanodont ancestor and migrated to what are now North and South America and Europe. An incredible evolutionary success, at one point during the Cretaceous, Hadrosaurs made up about 75 percent of all land animals.

For the most part, physical differences between the Hadrosaurine and Lambeosaurine branches of the family were minimal. With powerful rear legs twice as long as the front, all were primarily bipedal, but they undoubtedly dropped to all fours for more leisurely browsing on low-growing plants. As with their probable ancestor, Camptosaurus, this is evident from the hooves on the fingers of the hands as well as the toes of the feet. Unlike Camptosaurus, however, there were only three toes and four fingers. A laterally flattened, stiffened tail was carried horizontally off the ground to act as a counterbalance to the body mass when walking on just the hind legs. In this position, Hadrosaurs were capable of running quite fast.

Although these were gentle planteaters, Hadrosaurs possessed more teeth than any other type of dinosaur. Described as prism or chisel shaped, these existed in multiple rows, top and bottom, along the sides of the mouth. As they wore out, they were constantly replaced with new ones that emerged from beneath. There were, however, no teeth in the front of the mouth. Instead, there was a sharp, horny beak. Hadrosaurs also had cheek pouches for storing and controlling food while chewing.

We are fortunate in having "mummified" Hadrosaurs, from which it is possible to determine what the skin looked like. It is generally described as "pebbly," similar to the covering of a football. It was not scaly or horny like that of a modern reptile. The bumps on the backs and other more exposed areas of these creatures were larger than those on the stomach regions. It is felt by some that this difference in size may also be indicative of a difference in color between these areas. A very interesting Hadrosaur feature found on these mummies is that the fingers on the forelimbs were webbed.

While all of the above characteristics are typical of Hadrosaurs in general, one feature that distinguished Lambeosaurus from all the rest was its immense size. Possibly reaching a length of almost fifty feet, it was not only the largest member of its family, but also the largest Ornithopod.

Few major differences existed between the two Hadrosaur subfamilies. Lambeosaurines, which included Corythosaurus, Tsintaosaurus, and Parasaurolophus, as well as Lambeosaurus, are differentiated from Hadrosaurines by having somewhat shorter, sturdier arms and legs; higher spines on the pelvic vertebrae; and larger "bills." The lower jaws, however, were shorter, and the mouth possessed a noticeable downward curve to the front.

The most obvious difference between the two family branches was seen on the heads. Whereas Hadrosaurines had relatively small, solid crests or were crestless, Lambeosaurines possessed large, elaborate, hollow crests. The crests of each genus or species were quite distinctive in form. That of Lambeosaurus is described as hatchet shaped. Basically, a main, squarish portion angled forward over the brow, while a spikelike protrusion at the back projected rearward. It is possible this rear projection supported a decorative neck frill. These hollow crests were actually complex extensions of the nasal passages, the arrangement of which dictated the shape. Their purpose constitutes one of the two main controversies surrounding Lambeosaurine Hadrosaurs.

A number of explanations for the crests have appeared over the years. Because it was initially believed that Lambeosaurines were amphibious and spent a large portion of their time swimming and diving for food, it was thought the crests acted as aqualungs holding a reserve air supply or they were part of a snorkeling system that allowed the animals to keep breathing while eating underwater. Neither of these explanations stands up to scrutiny. There were no holes in the crests to allow their use as snorkels, and the minimal amount of extra air they may have held would have been of no value to creatures of their size. Furthermore, the very idea that these animals led aquatic lifestyles has been seriously challenged; more on this later.

Those who maintain Lambeosaurs were cold-blooded suggest that the crests, with their labyrinths of air channels, served as cooling devices for their brains. Essentially, air could circulate around the head, allowing heat to evaporate and keeping the brain the same temperature as body areas with deeper tissues.

Other solutions to the mystery of the crests are that they served various identification purposes. It was once believed in some circles that, like the lion's mane, only males had crests. Although this has been disproved, it is still thought by some that there were differences in crest size and shape between males and females and between adults and young. A third party maintains they served to identify members of one species from another. Different Lambeosaurine types undoubtedly lived in close proximity to each other and frequently mingled.

Another current opinion is that the hollow crests allowed these animals to keep breathing while simultaneously eating. Of course, this implies Lambeosaurs were constantly feeding and large amounts of food were consumed. This would, in turn, indicate a warm-blooded metabolism.

There are two final theories now in vogue with much to support them. First, it is held that the crests were resonating chambers that increased the loudness and depth of bellows uttered during the mating season or in times of danger. The other theory is that the crests may have helped enhance the sense of smell. In combination with apparently keen eyesight and hearing, this would have functioned as part of an excellent early warning system against predators.

Of course, the above arguments are not exclusive of each other. The crests may have aided breathing, acted as resonating devices for calling, served as identifying features, and increased the sense of smell, all at the same time.

The second debate about Hadrosaurs in general concerns the type of terrain they lived in. It was originally maintained that these were amphibious creatures that, living in swamps and along rivers and lakes, swam about and ate water plants. This belief was founded on the facts that the fingers were webbed and the snout resembled that of a duck. In essence, it was thought that any animal with such physical traits surely must have swum. Supporting this opinion was the broad, laterally flattened tail, which, it was felt, was swept from side to side to propel Hadrosaurs through the water.

Several major arguments have been put forward challenging the idea of an aquatic lifestyle. To begin with, only the smaller, weaker hands were webbed. One would expect the powerful rear feet to possess this attribute as well if the animals were truly amphibious. Also, it has been shown that the lateral spines on the tail vertebrae were not sufficient for the attachment of strong muscles required to swish the tail back and forth in a propelling motion. Furthermore, the stiffening rods that maintained the tail horizontally off the ground when walking would have prevented it from moving in the undulating manner necessary for swimming.

The most convincing argument against Hadrosaurs having been amphibious centers on their highly specialized teeth. These were designed for chewing coarse, tough food, not soft, mushy water plants. That this was the case was confirmed by the stomach contents of the Hadrosaur "mummies," which showed that pine needles, twigs, leaves, and seeds made up their diet. This being the situation, it is now maintained by most that Hadrosaurs were upland dwellers. This is not to say they did not enter the water and could not swim. It is quite likely that, if necessary, they were capable of swimming, but swimming was not a general practice, nor was it conducted with the efficiency once thought.

It is now possible to make some comments about the lifestyles and social habits of Hadrosaurs in general and Lambeosaurus in particular. These were upland grazing animals that lived in herds and, like Camptosaurus, held a place in the ecosystem similar to deer and antelope today. Also like Camptosaurus, their only defense was safety in numbers and their ability to detect the presence of predators early on, giving them time to make a speedy getaway.

A major Hadrosaur discovery is that they apparently cared for their young and established nurseries for this purpose. Such a site was found in 1979 in Montana. This consisted of what were large mud nests formed at fairly regular intervals. Mound shaped, these were about 10 feet (3.05 meters) in diameter and 5 feet (1.525 meters) in height, each having a saucerlike depression in the top. One of the nests contained the remains of eleven young Hadrosaurs, each about 1 meter long. From the wear on their teeth, it was clear they were not hatchlings. They obviously had stayed together in the nest as a group for some time. This supports the idea that after forming the nest and laying the eggs, the adults remained to protect and perhaps bring food to the newborn. This, in turn, implies a rather complex social structure for these beasts.

REQUIRED MATERIALS

Body: One $17^1/2$ x $4^1/4$ x $3/4$-inch piece of stock
Rear legs: Two 12 x $2^1/2$ x $3/4$-inch pieces of stock
Front legs: Two $8^3/4$ x $1^1/2$ x $3/4$-inch pieces of stock
Crest: One 2 x $1^1/2$ x $1/4$-inch piece of stock
Other: Four $3/8$-inch-diameter axle pegs for front and rear legs

BODY CONSTRUCTION

To construct a Lambeosaurus body, follow the same basic instructions as per Camptosaurus, except where otherwise noted.

Step 1.
Follow Steps 1 to 6 for the Camptosaurus, with the exception that a $3/8$-inch brad-point bit should be used to drill both the arm and leg holes through the body (see figs. L1 and L2).

Step 2.
With a $3/16$-inch brad-point bit, at an angle perpendicular to the side of the body, drill the eye holes $1/16$ inch deep. (see figs. L2 and L3).

Step 3.
With a $1/8$-inch brad-point bit, at the center point of the round and at a 45-degree angle to the side of the body, drill the nostril holes to a depth of $1/8$ inch (see figs. L2 and L3).

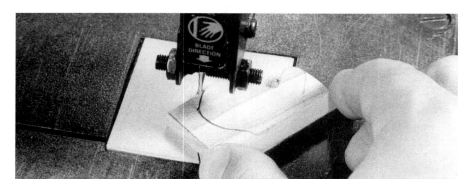

Step 4.
Lay out the crest pattern (see fig. L4) with the grain running from front to back.

Step 5.
Use a band saw to cut out the crest.

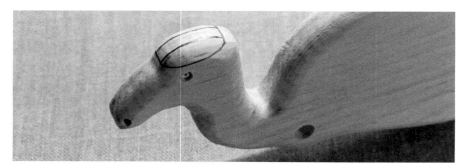

Step 6.
With a pencil, mark the area along the top centerline of the head to be removed to accommodate the crest (see fig. L4).

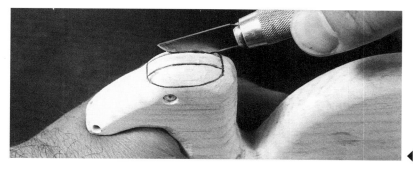

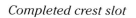
Completed crest slot

◀ **Cut #1**

◀ **Cut #2**

Step 7.
Using a small, narrow, straight chisel and/or a modeling knife, remove the wood within the marked area to the designated depth. The end result should be a shallow slot with parallel, vertical sides and flat bottom running along the centerline of the top of the head from front to back. This is best achieved gradually, alternating parallel, vertically downward cuts (cut #1 in fig. L4) to score the front-to-back lines, with horizontal cuts (cut #2) to remove the undesired wood in between. Be careful not to make the slot too wide. A snug fit is required for the crest.

Step 8.
Fit the crest to the slot. If the crest is too thick, fine-sand it to reduce its sides until it does fit.

Step 9.
With medium-grit sandpaper, sand out any irregularities in the body caused by cutting or routering.
Step 10.
Mark and carve the mouth using the Type A method described for the Camptosaurus (see fig. L5).
Step 11.
Fine-sand the body and the crest.
Step 12.
Glue the crest to the body, being careful not to get any glue on what will be exposed surfaces.

FRONT AND REAR LEG CONSTRUCTION
Both pairs of legs are made using the Type A construction method (see figs. L6 and L7).

Step 1.
Use a $^3/_8$-inch brad-point bit to drill the holes through all four legs for the axle pegs.
Step 2.
Router the designated areas on all four legs with a $^3/_8$-inch round-over bit.

Step 3.
Exclusive of the thickness of the heads, cut the four axle pegs to a length of $1^1/_8$ inches.

FINISHING AND ASSEMBLY
Step 1.
Finish as desired.
Step 2.
Assemble as per basic Type A leg construction.

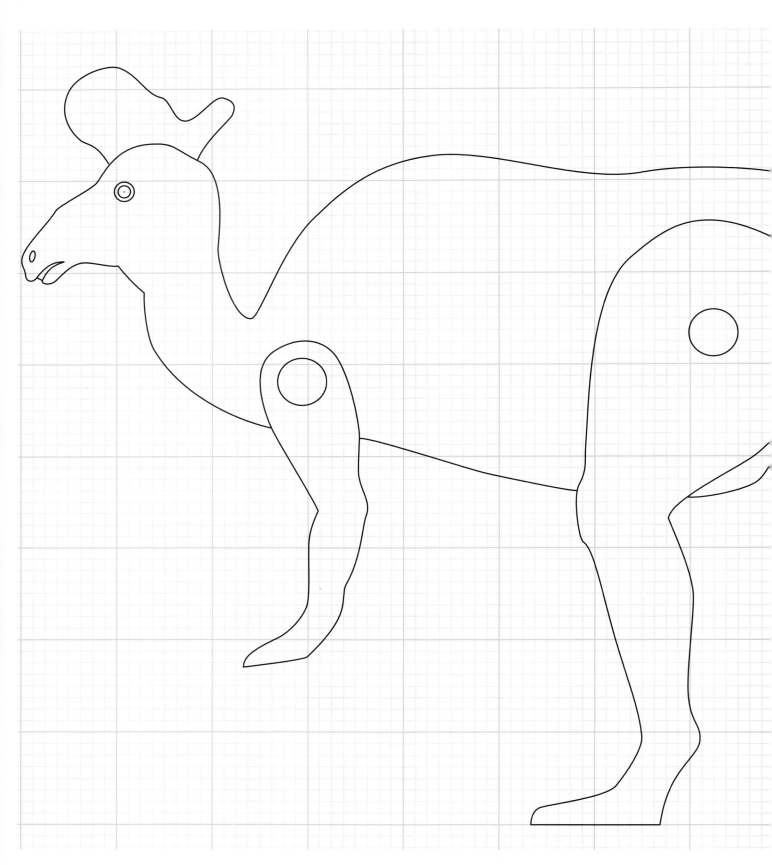

FIGURE L1. PLAN OF COMPLETED LAMBEOSAURUS (FULL-SCALE)

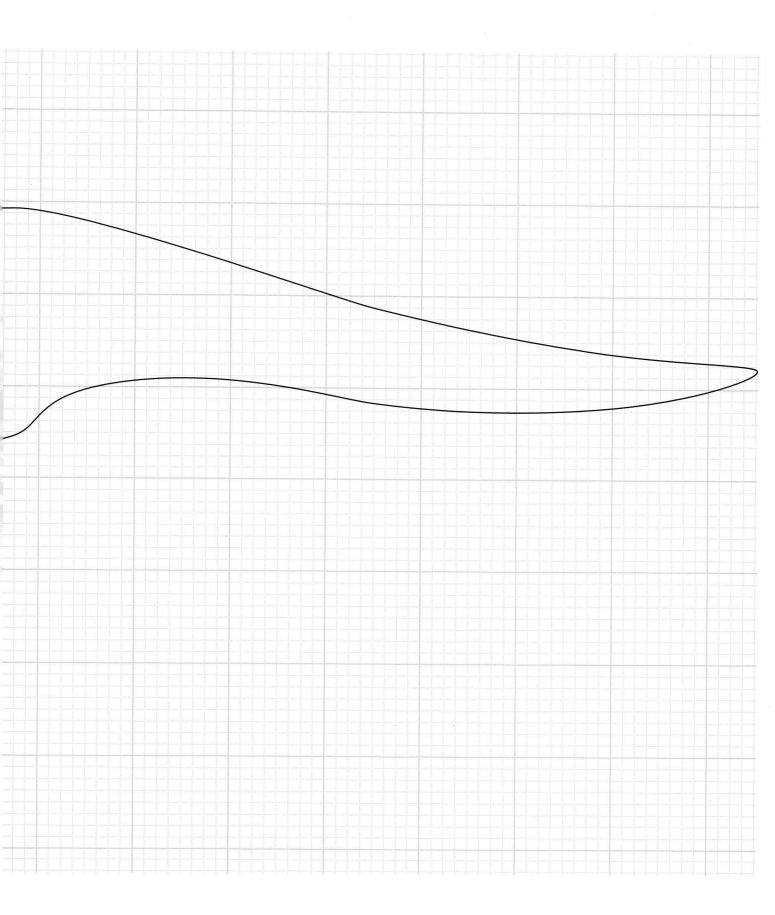

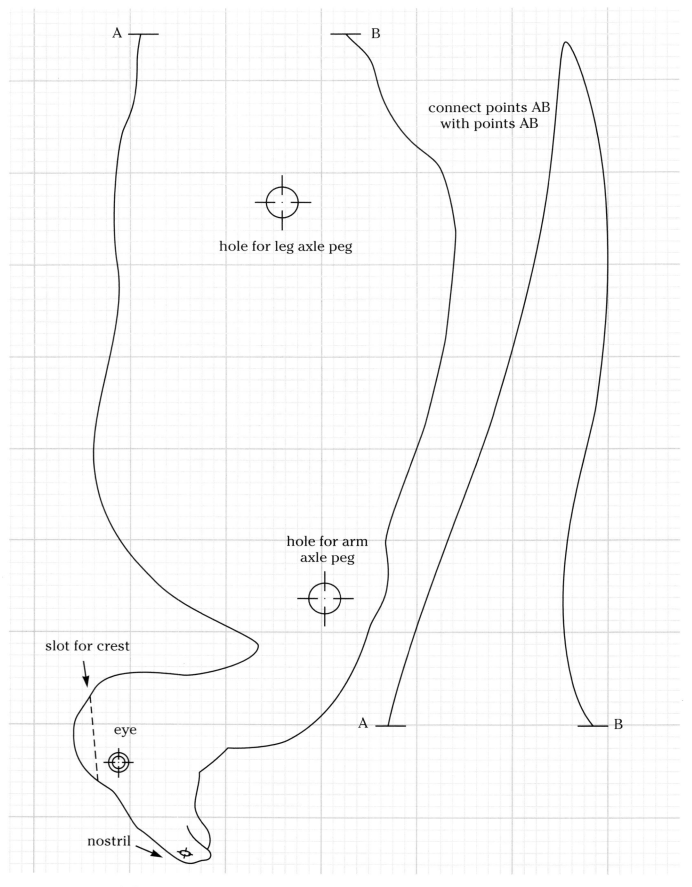

A

B

connect points AB
with points AB

hole for leg axle peg

hole for arm
axle peg

slot for crest

eye

A

B

nostril

FIGURE L2. LAMBEOSAURUS BODY PLAN (FULL-SCALE)

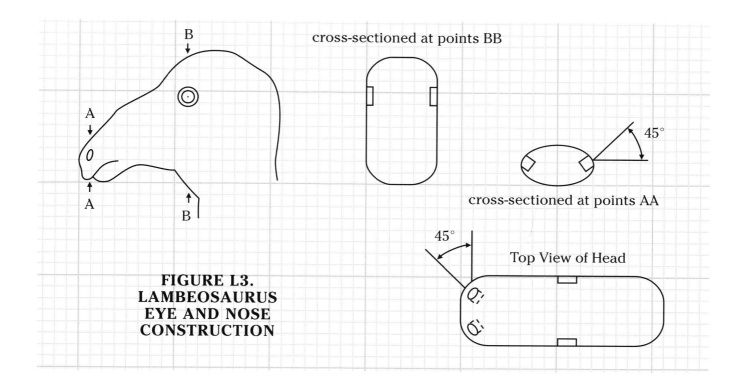

cross-sectioned at points BB

45°

cross-sectioned at points AA

45°

Top View of Head

**FIGURE L3.
LAMBEOSAURUS
EYE AND NOSE
CONSTRUCTION**

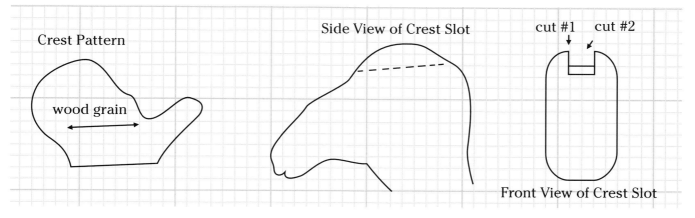

Crest Pattern

wood grain

Side View of Crest Slot

cut #1   cut #2

Front View of Crest Slot

FIGURE L4. LAMBEOSAURUS CREST CONSTRUCTION

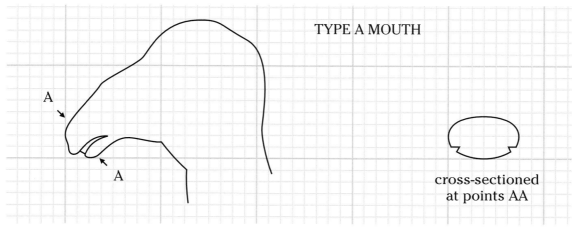

TYPE A MOUTH

cross-sectioned
at points AA

FIGURE L5. CARVING THE LAMBEOSAURUS MOUTH

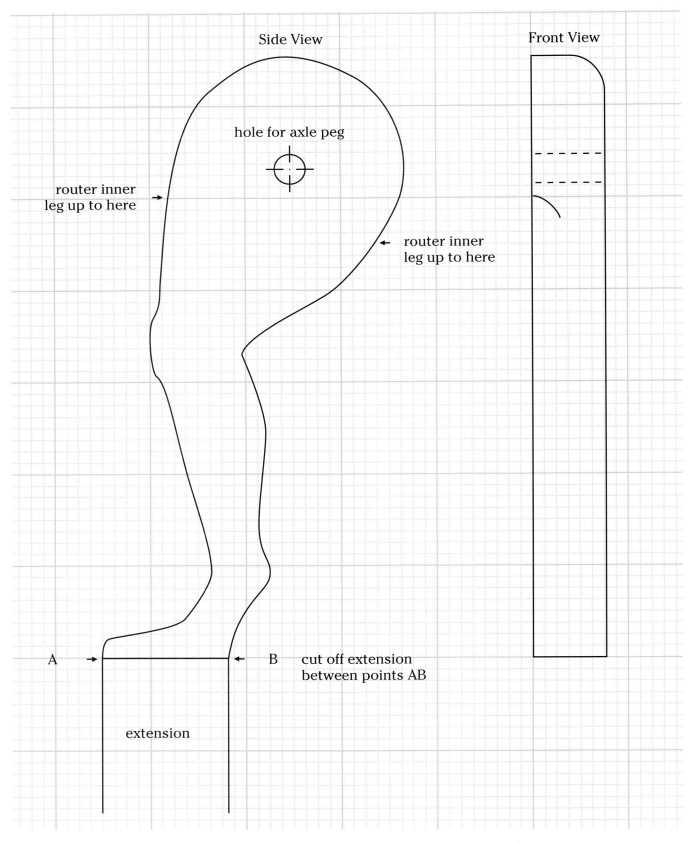

Side View

Front View

hole for axle peg

router inner
leg up to here

→ router inner
leg up to here

A →

← B   cut off extension
between points AB

extension

FIGURE L6. LAMBEOSAURUS REAR LEG PATTERN

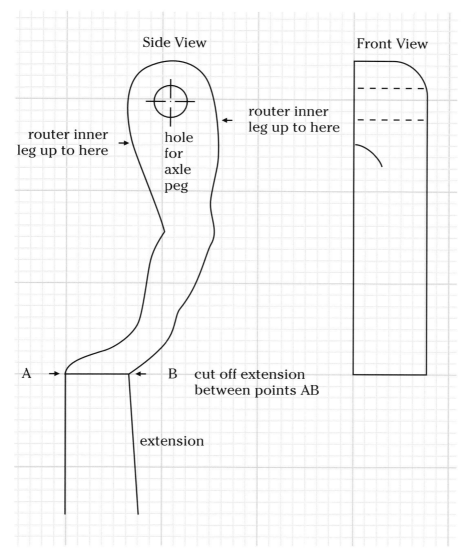

Side View

Front View

router inner
leg up to here

hole
for
axle
peg

router inner
leg up to here

A   B   cut off extension
between points AB

extension

FIGURE L7. LAMBEOSAURUS ARM PATTERN

Corythosaurus casuarius

Corythosaurus (Ko-RITH-uh-sawr-us):
"Helmeted lizard"
Order: Ornithischia, "bird-hipped"
Suborder: Ornithopoda, "bird-footed"
Infraorder: Iguanodontia
Family: Hadrosauridae
Subfamily: Lambeosaurine
Genus: *Corythosaurus*
Species: *Corythosaurus casuarius*

Close relatives: Lambeosaurus, Parasaurolophus,
Hypacrosaurus, and Tsintaosaurus
Length: Roughly 33 feet (10 meters)
Weight: 2 to 4.2 tons (1.8 to 3.8 metric tons)

The first fossils of Corythosaurus were found in 1912 by Barnum Brown and were first officially described in 1914. The original remains came from the Late or Upper Cretaceous Oldman (Belly River) Formation, Red Deer River, Alberta, Canada.

Since then, additional skeletons have been discovered in Montana and Baja California.

The roughly two dozen existing Corythosaurus skulls make this dinosaur very well known and provide a good sample for comparison. The shape of the

crest is what gave this creature its name, which means "helmeted lizard." From the skull openings, it has been determined that the males of this species had larger crests than the females. The crests of Corythosaurus juveniles were smaller still and grew with age.

Apart from the shape of the crest, a smaller size, and the belief by some that these animals lived in forest areas, Corythosaurus was very similar to Lambeosaurus. The general information supplied on Hadrosaurs in the previous chapter is applicable to Corythosaurus as well.

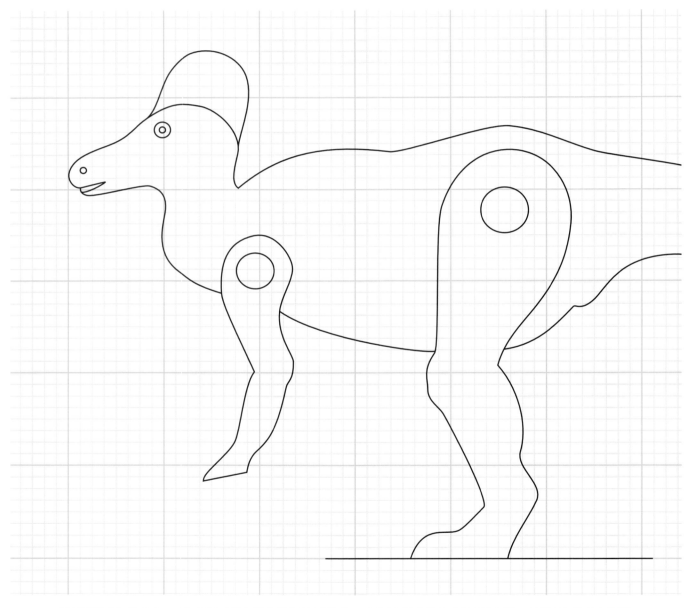

FIGURE CO1. PLAN OF COMPLETED CORYTHOSAURUS (FULL-SCALE)

REQUIRED MATERIALS

Body: One $11^1/_2$ x $3^1/_2$ x $^3/_4$-inch piece of stock
Crest: One $1^1/_2$ x $1^1/_2$ x $^1/_4$-inch piece of stock
Rear legs: Two $8^1/_2$ x 2 x $^3/_4$-inch pieces of stock
Front legs: Two 6 x $1^1/_4$ x $^3/_4$-inch pieces of stock
Other: Two $^1/_4$-inch-diameter axle pegs for the front legs and two
  $^3/_8$-inch-diameter axle pegs for the rear legs

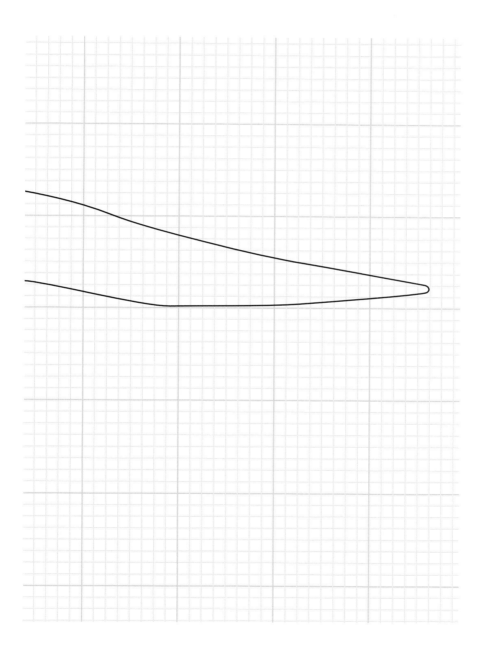

CORYTHOSAURUS CONSTRUCTION

The Corythosaurus model is constructed using exactly the same procedures as for the Lambeosaurus. The only differences are in the sizes of the various bits employed and the angles of the eye and nostril holes (see figs. CO2 through CO6).

- Use a $^1/_4$-inch-diameter brad-point bit to drill the holes for the front legs.
- Use a $^3/_8$-inch-diameter brad-point bit to drill the holes for the rear legs.
- Use a $^3/_{16}$-inch-diameter brad-point bit to drill the eye holes.
- Use a $^1/_{16}$-inch-diameter drill bit to drill the nostrils.
- Drill the eye and nostril holes at a 90-degree angle to the side of the head.
- Use a $^3/_8$-inch round-over bit for all routering.
- Exclusive of the thickness of the heads, cut all four axle pegs to a length of $1^1/_8$ inches.

Corythosaurus casuarius • **45**

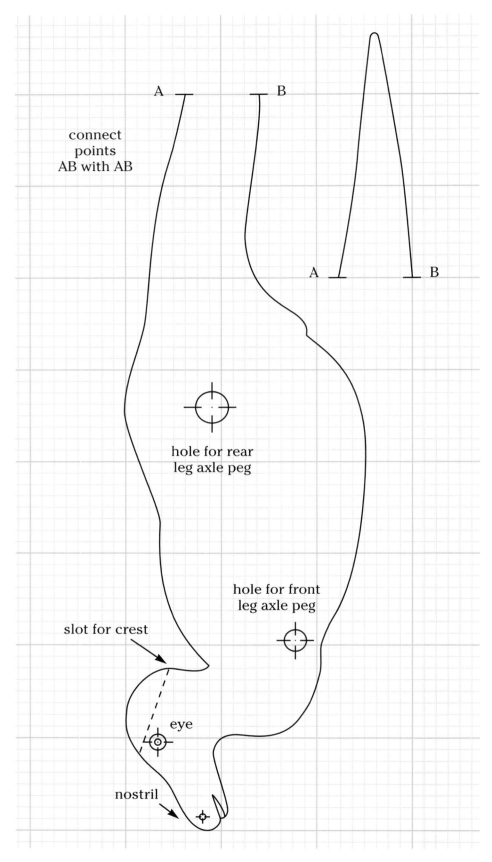

connect
points
AB with AB

hole for rear
leg axle peg

hole for front
leg axle peg

slot for crest

eye

nostril

FIGURE CO2. BODY PATTERN FOR CORYTHOSAURUS (FULL-SCALE)

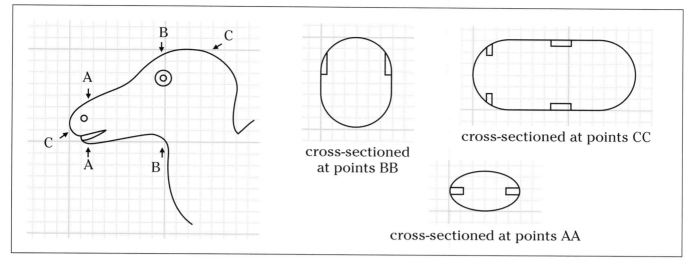

FIGURE CO3. CORYTHOSAURUS EYE AND NOSTRIL CONSTRUCTION

cross-sectioned
at points BB

cross-sectioned at points CC

cross-sectioned at points AA

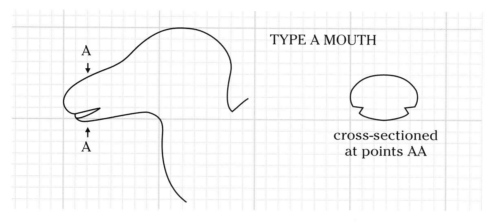

TYPE A MOUTH

cross-sectioned
at points AA

FIGURE CO4. CARVING THE CORYTHOSAURUS MOUTH

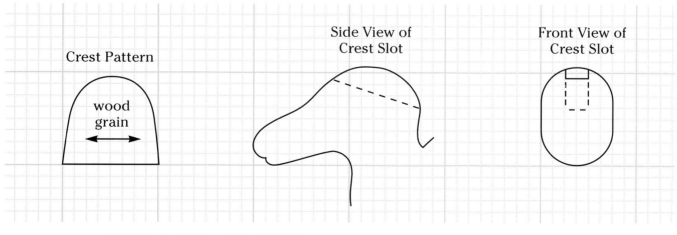

Crest Pattern

wood
grain

Side View of
Crest Slot

Front View of
Crest Slot

FIGURE CO5. CORYTHOSAURUS CREST CONSTRUCTION

REAR LEG PATTERN

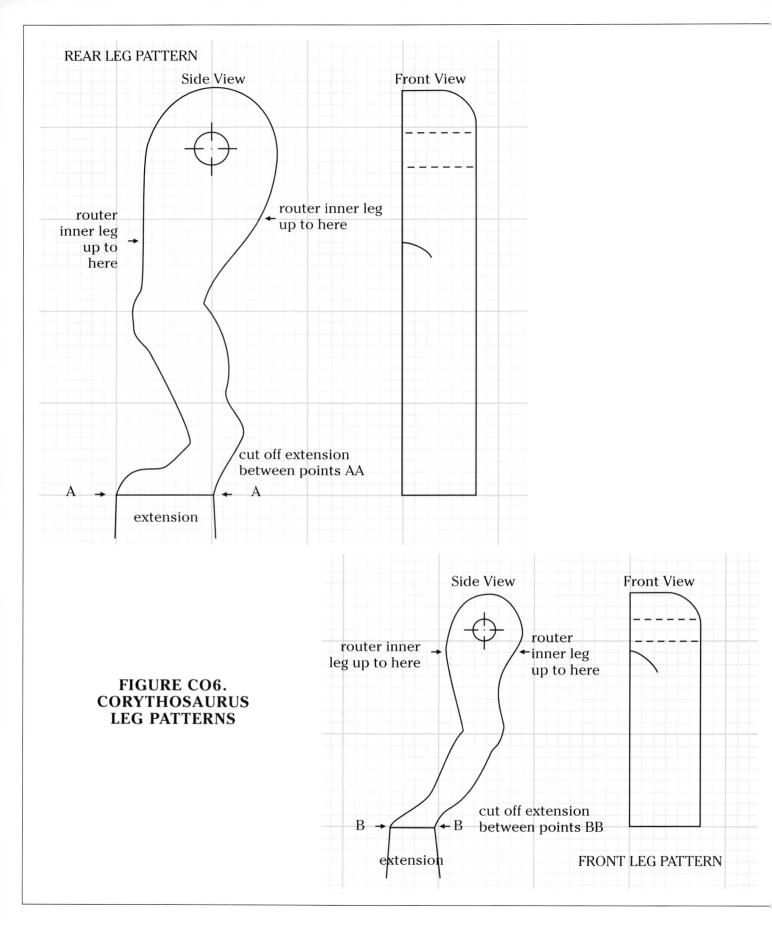

Side View

Front View

router
inner leg
up to
here

router inner leg
up to here

cut off extension
between points AA

A → ← A

extension

FIGURE CO6.
CORYTHOSAURUS
LEG PATTERNS

Side View

Front View

router inner
leg up to here

router
inner leg
up to here

cut off extension
between points BB

B → ← B

extension

FRONT LEG PATTERN

Ornithomimus velox

Ornithomimus (or-nith-uh-MY-mus): "Bird mimic"

Class: Reptilia	or	Archosauria	
Subclass: Diapsida	or	Dinosauria	
Superorder: Archosauria	or	Theropoda	
Order: Saurischia	or	Avetheropoda	
Suborder: Theropoda	or	Protoavia	
Infraorder: Ornithomimosauria			
Family: Ornithomimidae		Ornithomimidae*	
Subfamily: Ornithomiminae			
Genus: *Ornithomimus* without *Struthiomimus*, etc.	or	*Ornithomimus* with *Struthiomimus*, etc.	
Species: *Ornithomimus velox*		*Ornithomimus velox*	

Close relatives: Dromiceiomimus and Struthiomimus
Length: Up to 15 feet (4.5 meters)
Height: Up to 8 feet (2.5) meters at the hip

Note: Some authorities consider these animals a family within the infraorder Coelurosauria.

*O*rnithomimus velox is known from several incomplete skeletons, the first of which was unearthed by Othniel Marsh in 1890. This Upper Cretaceous dinosaur is found in the Denver Formation of Colorado and the Kaiparowits Formation of Utah. As is apparent from the classifications outlined above, there is debate over Ornithomimid taxonomy. While some consider Ornithomimus,

Dromiceiomimus, and Struthiomimus to represent distinctive genera, others believe they are merely variant species of the same genus. Whatever the case, differences between them were minimal. At the same time, some see Ornithomimids as a family evolved from Coelophysid ancestors of Coelurosauria stock, and others uphold that they deserve their own infraorder apart from Coelurosaurs.

Physically, the graceful Ornithomimids in general and *Ornithomimus velox* in particular were the most birdlike of all dinosaurs. Except for the fact they had tails and arms with hands instead of wings, they strongly resembled modern ostriches. As with other bipedal dinosaurs, the relatively long tail was stiffened and carried horizontally off the ground to act as a counterbalance for the torso, long flexible neck, and small head. The rear legs upon which the body sat were long and slender, but powerful. Three forward-extending toes were present on each foot, but the rearward one found on other Theropods had disappeared. The arms, too, were long, but nowhere near the length of the legs. Despite the lack of an opposable thumb, the three long, clawed fingers were quite capable of effective grasping. The bones in the limbs and elsewhere were hollow like those of birds.

Although the head was small and the skull was fairly fragile, the brain was quite large, comparable in relative size to that of an ostrich. This means that these creatures were among the most intelligent of all dinosaurs. *Ornithomimus velox* also had very large eyes, allowing excellent eyesight. The eyes were set to be partially binocular, further enhancing their vision. The eyes were somewhat flattened, however, so they could not be rolled. The animal had to turn its head from side to side to see everything that was going on around it. Although this dinosaur had excellent vision and brainpower, it is believed that its sense of smell was not very advanced.

Another way in which *Ornithomimus velox* differed from other Theropods is that they did not have teeth. Instead, there was a sharp, powerful horn-covered beak.

One thing paleontologists generally agree upon about Ornithomimids is that they were very agile and fast. This is so apparent from the graceful build and long, powerful legs with an extremely high shin-to-thigh length ratio, that even proponents of cold-bloodedness offer little argument against these animals having been speedy. Still, the very nature of their build combined with their hollow bones tends

to support that they were, in fact, warm-blooded. In any case, it is estimated that springing along on their long toes, Ornithomimids could move as fast as 50 miles per hour. As such, they have been described as one of the fastest animals of all time and the "veritable gazelle of the dinosaur world."

One feature of Ornithomimids that is debated among scientists, especially between proponents of warm- and cold-bloodedness, is what the skin surface looked like. While most, regardless of camp, feel there was no covering, some believers in warm-bloodedness speculate that these dinosaurs may have had feathers.

Another aspect of Ornithomimids that is not readily agreed upon is their diet. This is primarily because the toothless beak, speed-oriented build, and grasping hands indicate a highly specialized animal. The lack of teeth supports that, unlike other Theropods, these creatures were not active predators. Instead, it is commonly believed that although they were still omnivorous, they had reverted to a primarily herbivorous diet. In essence, while mainly eating plants, seeds, and fruit, they occasionally supplemented their diet with insects and the occasional small animal. Many who believe they were omnivorous think that eggs constituted a major food source too. The eating of eggs may explain Ornithomimus's combination of interesting physical attributes. Basically, it could quickly run up to the nest of another dinosaur, snatch an egg in its hands, make a speedy escape, and crack the egg open with its beak to get at the contents. An alternative line of thought is that these creatures lived along shorelines, where they waded for shellfish. The long toes would support them in soft mud while groping for shellfish, which they would crack open with their beaks. It has been shown, however, that the toes could not expand wide enough to support the animal on soft surfaces. Most recently, it has been asserted that they had evolved into true herbivores and no longer ate any meat at all. They used their hands to hold branches and pull them toward their mouths to be clipped off with their sharp beaks.

From their large brains, it is thought that Ornithomimus was capable of a fairly complex social structure. They probably lived in herds or flocks, and one authority suggests that they may have been capable of vocal interaction. It is believed that the young, hatched from eggs, were probably fairly advanced at birth. Still, they were cared for by adults. Speed was the Ornithomimids' best defense against predators, but if cornered, they were capable of pecking, biting, and kicking. Exactly what type of terrain they lived in is yet another debated question. Some believe they inhabited open plains while others contend that they lived in dense, dark forests and swamps. Perhaps it depended on the particular species of the Ornithomimid.

REQUIRED MATERIALS

Body: One $5^1/2$ x 2 x $^1/2$-inch piece of stock, plus extra material for a 4-inch extension off the end of the tail

Rear legs: Two 8 x $1^3/4$ x $^1/2$-inch pieces of stock

Arms: Two 2 x $^1/2$ x $^3/8$-inch pieces of stock

Other: Two $^1/4$-inch-diameter axle pegs and one 1-inch length of $^1/8$-inch-diameter dowel rod

---

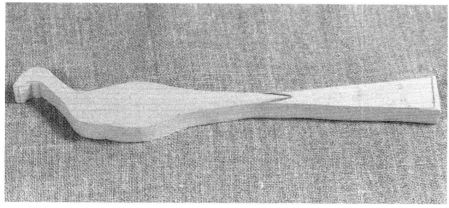

Ornithomimus cutout with tail extension

BODY CONSTRUCTION
Step 1.
Lay out the body pattern as with the previous dinosaurs, but allow for enough extra stock to add a 4-inch extension off the end of the tail (see figs. O1 and O2). This body pattern and a few others that follow are somewhat small, and as with legs, the extension will serve as a handle during the routering process.

Step 2.
Follow Steps 2 and 3 as per Camptosaurus (see fig. O2).
Step 3.
Use a $^1/4$-inch round-over bit to router both sides of the body, routering only those areas designated in the pattern (see fig. O2). Do not router the bulge over the eyes. If you feel uncomfortable routering close to this point, stop short of it and trim or carve off the excess, and round in with a modeling knife.
Step 4.
With a $^1/4$-inch brad-point bit, drill the rear leg hole at a 90-degree angle through the body.

Step 5.
With a $^1/8$-inch brad-point bit, drill the front arm hole at a 90-degree angle through the body.
Step 6.
With a $^1/8$-inch brad-point bit, drill the eye holes perpendicular to the side of the body to a depth of $^1/16$ inch (see figs. O2 and O3).

Step 7.
At the designated points on top of the nose (see figs. O2 and O3), make the nostrils by merely inserting a heavy-gauge pin or awl about $1/16$ inch and rotating it a little to open up small holes. A hand-held drill with a $1/32$-inch bit can be used to do this, but it is awkward.

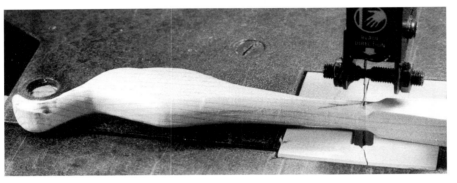

Step 8.
Now use a band saw to cut off the tail extension and finish shaping the tip of the tail.

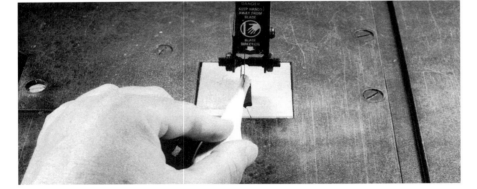

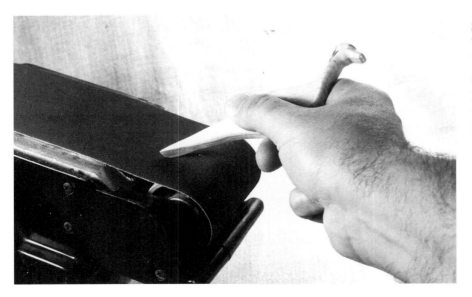

Step 9.
With a belt sander, taper the tail a bit by removing wood from the sides only. When sufficiently tapered, use the sander on the tip of the tail to re-create the round made with the router (see fig. O2).

CARVING THE MOUTH: TYPE B MOUTH

To carve the mouth of the Ornithomimus and some other dinosaurs that follow, a variation on the Type A method is used. Appropriately enough, this is called the Type B method. This is also created by a series of two basic cuts. Instead of creating a V-like notch in the side of the face, however, you will simply be removing some wood from the sides of the lower jaw. This will create the appearance of the upper jaw overhanging the lower. This same procedure will be used on Pachycephalosaurus, Plateosaurus, and Stegosaurus.

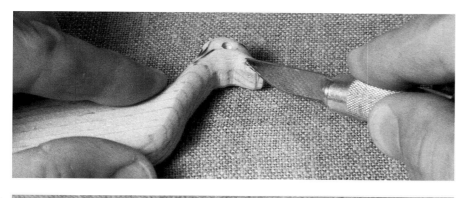

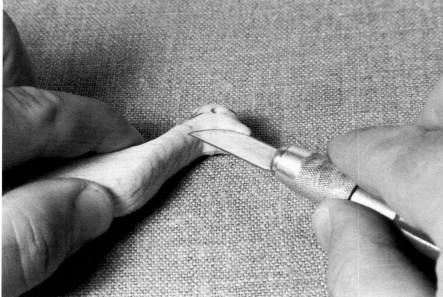

Step 1.

This procedure is identical to Step 1 for Type A mouths, with the exception that only the sides of the mouth are involved. There is no need to cut into the front area of the upper mouth (see fig. O4).

Step 2.

From beneath the jaw, make a series of upward cuts at a 90-degree angle with the first series along each side. Again, there is no need to make any cuts at the front of the lower jaw. Each cut should start at a point at the very sides, directly below the corners of the mouth (which the cuts themselves, when executed, should connect with), and taper in towards the chin to a maximum depth of $1/16$ inch. As with the Type A mouth, this second series of cuts should meet with the first, and the unwanted wood can just be lifted out.

Step 3.

If necessary, repeat the two previous steps in sequence.

Step 4.

By carving, sanding, or both, round in the sharp forward corners and bottom edges of the lower jaw. If possible, simulate the round made by the router bit elsewhere on the model.

Step 5.

With the knife or rifflers, even out any irregularities.

Completed Type B Mouth

Step 6.
Sand the areas from which the wood was removed.

Step 7.
Proceed as per Steps 9 and 10 for Camptosaurus.

REAR LEG CONSTRUCTION

The rear legs are made using the Type A construction method (see fig. O5).

Step 1.
Use a ¹⁄₄-inch brad-point bit to drill the holes through the legs for the axle pegs.

Step 2.
Router the designated areas with a ¹⁄₄-inch round-over bit.

Step 3.
Exclusive of the thickness of the head, cut the axle pegs to lengths of ³⁄₄ inch.

Step 4.
Proceed as per basic Type A leg construction, as described for Camptosaurus.

ARM CONSTRUCTION

The arms are made using the Type B construction method (see fig. O5). *Note:* Do not attempt to router these; they are too small.

Step 1.
To accommodate the dowel rod, use a ¹⁄₈-inch brad-point bit to drill a hole ¹⁄₈ inch deep on the inside of each arm. (see fig. O5)

Step 2.
Mark the spaces between the fingers on each hand with a pencil.

Step 3.
Using a band saw or scroll saw, cut small, narrow V notches to depths of ¹⁄₈ inch to remove the unwanted wood between the fingers.

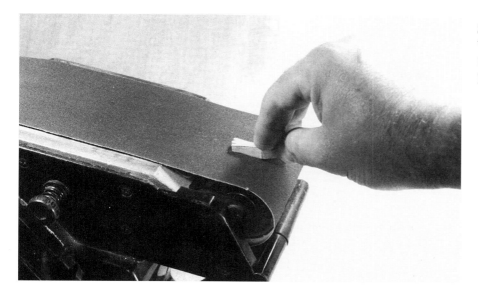

Step 4.
With a belt sander using a fine-grit belt, taper each side of the forward half of each arm.

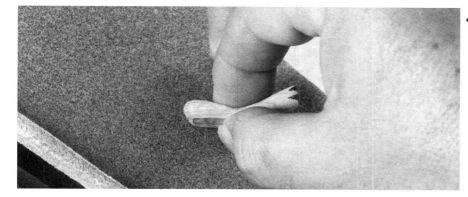

◀ **Step 5.**
By sanding, break the edges of the arms in the designated areas (especially over the shoulders) to round them out.

Step 6.
Cut the section of $\frac{1}{8}$-inch-diameter dowel rod to a length of $\frac{7}{8}$ inch.

Step 7.
Proceed as per basic Type B arm and leg construction.

FINISHING AND ASSEMBLY

Step 1.
Finish to taste.

Step 2.
Assemble as per basic Type A and B arm and leg construction.

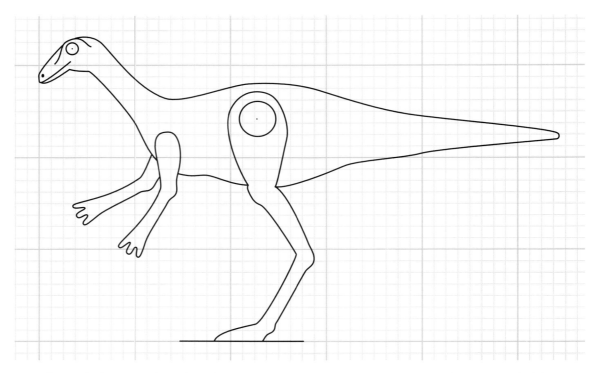

FIGURE O1. PLAN OF COMPLETED ORNITHOMIMUS (FULL-SCALE)

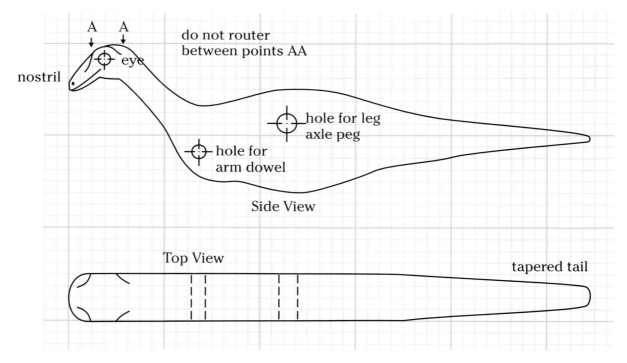

FIGURE O2. BODY PATTERN FOR ORNITHOMIMUS

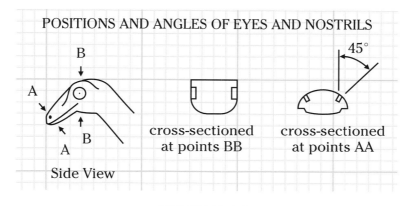

FIGURE O3.
ORNITHOMIMUS EYE AND NOSE CONSTRUCTION

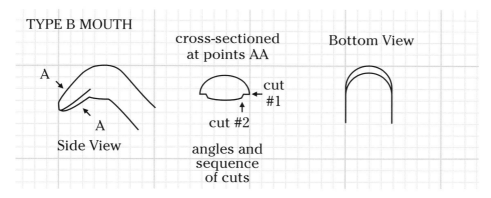

FIGURE O4.
CARVING THE ORNITHOMIMUS MOUTH

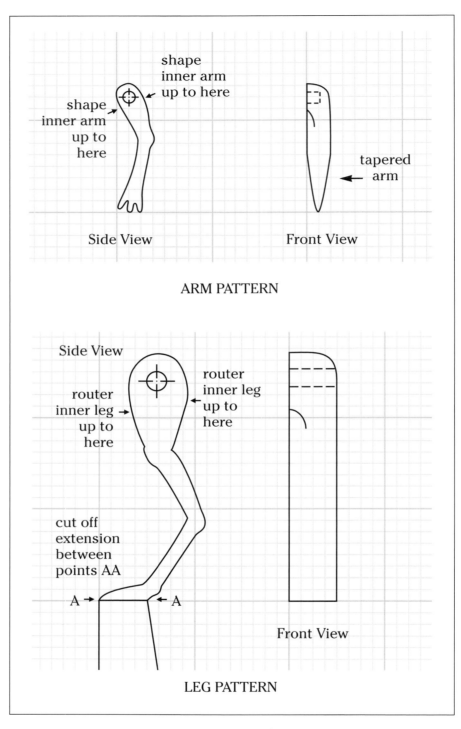

FIGURE O5.
ORNITHOMIMUS ARM AND LEG PATTERNS

Pachycephalosaurus grangeri

Pachycephalosaurus (Pak-ee-SEF-uh-lo-sawr-us):
"Thick-headed lizard"
Order: Ornithischia
Suborder: Ornithopoda or Pachycephalosauria
Family: Pachycephalosauridae
Genus: *Pachycephalosaurus*
Species: *Pachycephalosaurus grangeri*

Close relatives: Stegoceras and Prenocephale
Length: 15 to 18 feet (13.72 to 16.46 meters)
Height: About 6 ½ feet (5.95 meters) at the hip
Weight: 500 to 1,000 pounds

Members of this dinosaur family are collectively nick-named "bone heads," after their most distinctive physical feature, thick, knobby skulls. First discovered in 1902 in Montana's Upper Cretaceous Lance Formation, different types of Pachycephalosaurids also are known from Mongolia, China, Madagascar, and England. *Pachycephalosaurus grangeri*, specifically, comes from the Montana strata, and creatures that are similar, if not the same, are found in Wyoming and South Dakota.

A major question about Pachycephalosaurus concerns where they fit in the zoological classification.

Though most consider them a family within the suborder Ornithopoda, some prefer to place them in their own, altogether separate suborder, Pachycephalosauria. Those in the majority believe they evolved from ancestral Hypsilophodonts.

Pachycephalosaurus grangeri was the largest family member. Habitually bipedal, this animal walked with its back horizontal to the ground and its tail held straight out behind to counterbalance the body. Although the rear legs were clearly powerful, the speed of these creatures is debatable. Some believe they were fairly slow; others maintain they were

59

quite fast. There were five fingers on the hands and four toes on the feet. Despite their sharp teeth, Pachycephalosaurus was a docile planteater. Both the eyesight and sense of smell of the Pachycephalosaurus were very keen.

As noted, the most distinctive characteristic of this dinosaur was its thick skull. The dome of the Pachycephalosaurus could be as thick as 10 inches (25 centimeters), and it was formed of fibrous bony columns positioned perpendicularly to the outer surface. Wreathing the base of the skull and covering the snout were knobby spikes up to 5 inches (13 centimeters) in length. Based on these features is the generally held contention that the heads were used as rams. This opinion is supported by other physical attributes. The neck was designed to resist lateral bending, which, in association with the horizontally maintained spinal column, created a body structure capable of absorbing and withstanding serious shock. Indications are that males possessed thicker skulls than females. If so, we can acquire some understanding of the purpose of these heavy heads.

It is felt that Pachycephalosaurus lived in herds, and like modern herding animals, males probably dueled with each other for dominance of the group. This was done by butting heads, a relatively harmless procedure that resolved the issue. Their thick skulls and spikes may also have been used as defensive weapons against predators, but this is questionable. Another suggested use is that in order to escape predators, the head could be employed to smash down thick brush, allowing escape through heavy undergrowth.

One final physical feature of note is the incredibly wide hips possessed by Pachycephalosaurus. This has led to speculation that they gave live birth instead of laying eggs.

Pachycephalosaurs are known primarily from their skulls, which are frequently found in situations indicating that they were washed down watercourses from higher ground. This tends to suggest that they lived in hilly or even mountainous regions. Still, some authorities feel they inhabited open plains, and others uphold they dwelt on floodplains and in swamps. Wherever they lived, they were possibly a major food source for *Tyrannosaurus rex*.

REQUIRED MATERIALS

Body: One 5³/₄ x 2¹/₄ x ¹/₂-inch piece of stock, plus enough additional stock to include a 4-inch extension off the tail

Legs: Two 7¹/₂ x 1 x ¹/₂-inch pieces of stock

Arms: Two 1¹/₄ x ⁵/₈ x ¹/₄-inch pieces of stock

Other: Two ¹/₄-inch-diameter axle pegs for the legs, one 1-inch section of ¹/₈-inch- diameter dowel rod for the arms, and at least ten round toothpicks

---

BODY CONSTRUCTION

Step 1.
Follow Steps 1 to 3 as per Camptosaurus, and factor in extra wood off the end of the tail for an extension as with Ornithomimus (see fig. P2).

Step 2.
With a ¹/₄-inch round-over bit, router all edges of the body.

Step 3.
With a ¹/₄-inch brad-point bit, drill the rear leg hole at a 90-degree angle through the body.

Step 4.
With a ¹/₈-inch brad-point bit, drill the front arm hole at a 90-degree angle through the body.

Step 5.
With a ¹/₈-inch brad-point bit, perpendicular to the side of the body,

drill each eye hole to a depth of ¹/₁₆ inch (see figs. P2 and P3).

Step 6.
With a ¹/₁₆-inch bit at the center point of the round at the designated spot on the nose, and at an angle of 45 degrees with the side of the body, drill the two nostril holes to a depth of ¹/₁₆ inch each (see figs. P2 and P3).

Step 7.
Using only a pencil at first, mark the points on the back of the head and the nose for the holes for the knobs (see fig. P4).

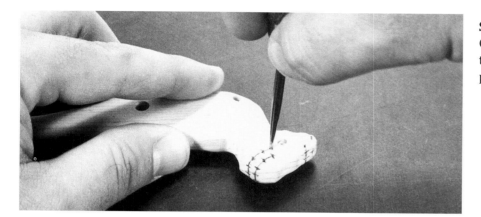

Step 8.
Once these points are determined to be evenly spaced and correctly positioned, mark them with an awl.

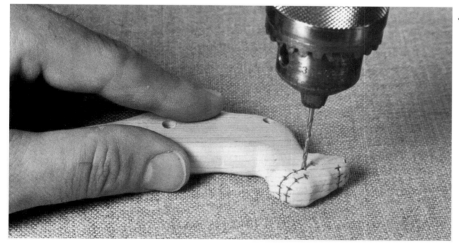

◀ **Step 9.**
With a ¹/₁₆-inch drill bit, drill each of the twenty holes for the knobs to a depth of ¹/₁₆ inch.

Step 10.
Sand the entire body to a fine finish at this time.

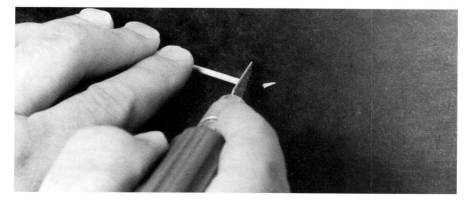

Step 11.
Take ten round toothpicks, and cut off the tips of each at the point where the diameter widens almost to ¹/₁₆ inch.

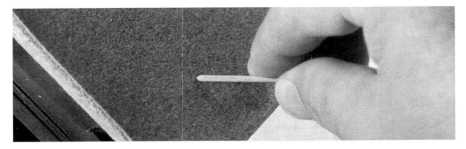

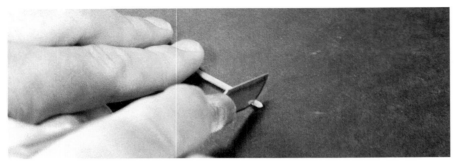

Step 12.
Use fine-grain sandpaper to round off the new ends of each toothpick.

Step 13.
With a modeling knife, cut off the ends of each toothpick ¹⁄₈ inch in from the new ends.

Step 14.
Now use a pin to apply a small amount of glue to the inside of each hole. Be careful not to get any on what will be exposed surfaces.

Step 15.
Insert a ¹⁄₈ inch length of prepared toothpick into each hole and let dry.

Step 16.
Mark and carve the mouth in accordance with the Type B method described for Ornithomimus.

LEG CONSTRUCTION

The legs are made using the Type A construction method (see fig. P5).

Step 1.
Use a ¹⁄₄-inch brad-point bit to drill the holes through the legs for the axle pegs.

Step 2.
With a ¹⁄₄-inch round-over bit, router the designated areas.

Step 3.
Exclusive of the thickness of the head, cut the two axle pegs to a length of ³⁄₄ inch.

ARM CONSTRUCTION

The arms are made using the Type B construction method (see fig. P5). *Note:* Do not attempt to router these; they are too small.

Step 1.
To accommodate the dowel rod, use a ¹⁄₈-inch brad-point bit to drill a hole ¹⁄₈ inch on the inside of each arm.

Step 2.
With a pencil, mark four evenly spaced, fanning lines on each hand to denote the spaces between what will be the fingers.

Step 3.
Now use a band saw or scroll saw to make four very narrow, ¹⁄₈-inch-deep V cuts along these lines to create the spaces between the fingers.

Step 4.
Using a belt sander with a fine-grit belt, taper the sides of the fore-arms only.

Step 5.
By sanding, break the edges of each arm in the designated areas (especially over the shoulders) to round them out.

Step 6.
Cut the section of ¹⁄₈-inch-diameter dowel rod to a length of ⁷⁄₈ inch.

FINISHING AND ASSEMBLY

Step 1.
Finish as desired.

Step 2.
Assemble as per basic Type A and B arm and leg construction.

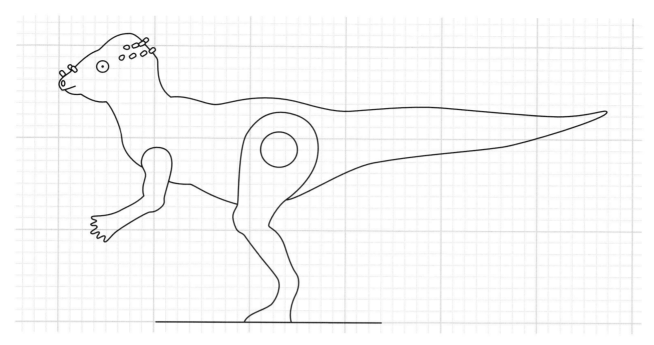

FIGURE P1. PLAN OF COMPLETED PACHYCEPHALOSAURUS (FULL-SCALE)

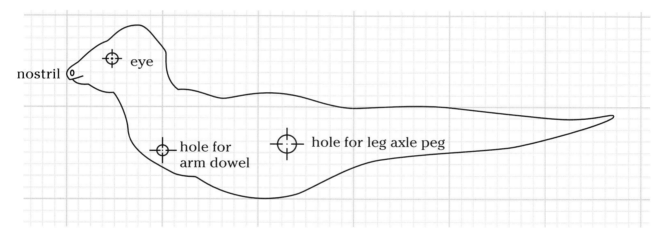

FIGURE P2. BODY PATTERN FOR PACHYCEPHALOSAURUS

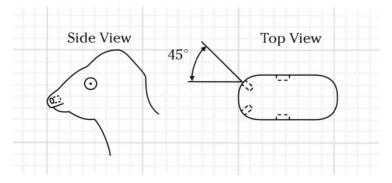

FIGURE P3. PACHYCEPHALOSAURUS EYE AND NOSE CONSTRUCTION

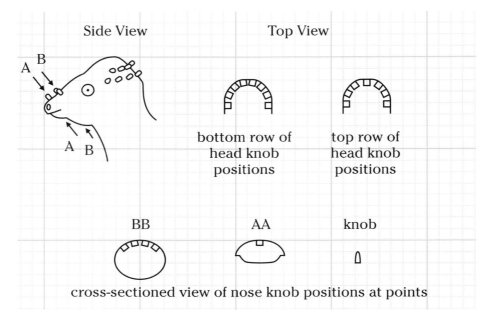

FIGURE P4. PACHYCEPHALOSAURUS KNOB CONSTRUCTION

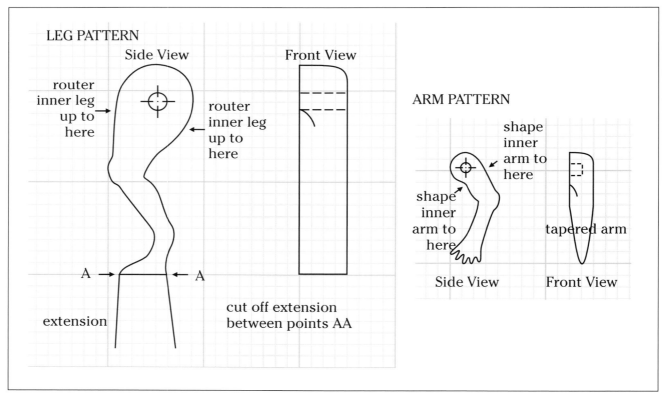

FIGURE P5. PACHYCEPHALOSAURUS LEG AND ARM PATTERNS

Tyrannosaurus rex

Tyrannosaurus rex (tye-RAN-uh-sawr-us rex): "King of the tyrant lizards" **Order:** Saurischia **Suborder:** Theropoda **Infraorder:** Carnosauria **Family:** Tyrannosauridae **Genus:** *Tyrannosaurus* **Species:** *Tyrannosaurus rex*	**Close relatives:** Tarbosaurus and Albertosaurus (Gorgosaurus) **Length:** 39 to 40 feet (12 meters) **Height:** About 18 ½ feet (5.6 meters) **Weight:** 6 to perhaps as much as 8 tons (about 5.44 to 7.26 metric tons)

*T*yrannosaurus rex, the largest meateater ever to walk the earth, marked the height of Carnosaur evolution. The very rare fossil remains of this animal, which lived during the Upper (Late) Cretaceous period, are found in the northern areas of western North America. The first were discovered in 1902 by Barnum Brown in the Hell Creek rock formations of Montana. Tyrannosaurus may, however, have roamed as far south as present-day southern Texas.

Like other dinosaurs, various aspects of the Tyrannosaurus's lifestyle and physical makeup are seri-

ously debated by paleontologists. One feature of its body about which opinions have changed, but over which there is seemingly little disagreement, is its tail. Early reconstructions and representations showed this beast with its tail dragging on the ground. As such, it acted as a prop that, with the two rear legs, created a tripod effect and helped maintain the balance of the body when standing. This resulted in a stance with the back poised at about a 45-degree angle with the ground. In fact, the tail was carried off the ground almost straight out behind, with the back

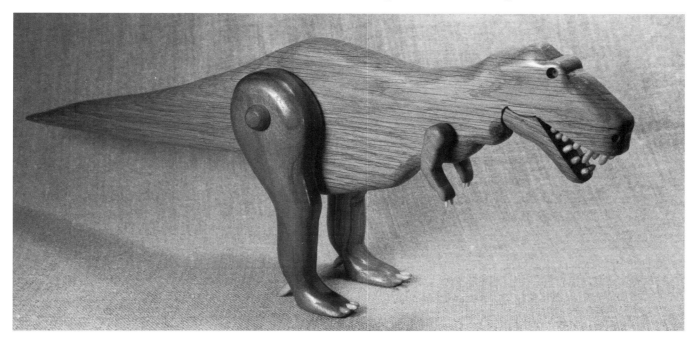

also in a roughly horizontal position. In essence, Tyrannosaurus balanced on its hind legs only, and the large tail acted as a counterweight for the mass of body extending in front of the rear legs.

While it is generally accepted that this is how the animal stood, there is serious debate over how it moved. Some authorities maintain it was slow and ponderous with a ducklike waddle, and could not exceed 3 or 4 miles per hour. Others insist that Tyrannosaurus was quick and agile and could run as fast as 45 miles per hour. This disagreement stems from differences of opinion about whether this creature was warm- or cold-blooded, and about the structure of the bones, joints, and muscles in the rear legs.

If cold-blooded, Tyrannosaurus would be capable only of short periods of slow movement. In conjunction, one authority believes that the nature of the muscles was such that the leg could not be extended very far. As a result, it could take only short steps and could not run. Others in this camp feel that the joints would have been unable to absorb the shock of fast movement.

In opposition, there are paleontologists who assert that the powerful legs were built for speed, capable of long strides, and able to withstand the stress. Also, they believe Tyrannosaurus was warm-blooded. It is argued that simply to stand, support its large body, and maintain its balance would require more energy than could be mustered if cold-blooded. Of course, any movement would require even more. Another belief is that the strong leg muscles would need a lot of exercise just to keep them in shape, and such frequent exertion would not be possible with a reptilianlike metabolism. There is no denying that the rear legs were powerfully muscled, and these muscles obviously served a distinct purpose.

The questions of fast versus slow and warm- versus cold-blooded lead to another. What were Tyrannosaurus's eating habits? The traditionalists who argue for cold-bloodedness and slow movement say that because of these very factors, the animal could not have been an active, aggressive hunter. It was simply not fast enough nor did it possess the energy to chase, catch, fight, and kill prey. Furthermore, if cold-blooded, it required relatively little food. Consequently, these paleontologists feel the fierce-looking Tyrannosaurus was actually a scavenger that fed off the bodies of dinosaurs killed by other, more active predators. Also, it is said that despite their wicked appearance, the 6-inch-long, serrated teeth were very

weak and would break off under the strain of using them in a fight.

The proponents of warm-bloodedness and speed counter with the argument that these features both allowed active hunting and necessitated it, because larger amounts of food were needed to maintain the metabolism. Basically, these scientists uphold that these were quick, powerful, and agile creatures, more than capable of stalking and grappling with a Hadrosaur or Ceratopsian in mortal combat. Also, they believe the teeth were quite strong, and even if they did break off, it was of little consequence, because they would be continually replaced with new ones. Like the modern shark, Tyrannosaurus had an endless supply of teeth. They also believe these were extremely aggressive animals because of the very advanced and powerful nature of the neck and jaw muscles in association with the massive head and large mouth. Obviously developed for active use, these features would be unnecessary for a mere scavenger. In addition, it is pointed out that the eye sockets had evolved to face toward the front, creating at least a degree of stereoscopic vision—something needed by predators engaged in active hunting and fighting, as it allows depth perception. Finally, it is shown in the fossil record that the ratio of predators to prey in the food chain of the prehistoric ecosystem was the same as with mammals, and not as with reptiles. Basically, there were comparatively more planteaters, because a lot of food was required to maintain a relatively small population of warm-blooded meateaters.

One of the most noticeable aspects of Tyrannosaurus is its tiny, 30-inch forearms with only two claws. Compared with those of other, earlier Carnosaurs, these appear deformed and virtually useless. It is said that a modern, healthy adult could win an arm-wrestling contest with one of these huge beasts. These arms could not be used to grasp, and they were too diminutive to be of any assistance when fighting. They did, however, serve a purpose, and this is something else paleontologists seem to agree on. When Tyrannosaurus slept, it probably did so on its stomach, or it at least had to first turn onto its stomach when it came time to stand up. Without arms and claws, however, it would not be able to get up, because if it would simply try to position its rear legs beneath itself to do so, they would merely scoot the beast along the ground on its chin. To raise itself up, it would dig the forearm claws into the ground to keep it from sliding forward while it walked the rear legs up beneath, allowing it to stand.

What about their social life? Again, this is open to question. Some maintain that Tyrannosaurs were solitary creatures; others believe they hunted in packs or family groups like modern wolves—a rather terrifying image! A long, horn-covered ridge running down the nose may indicate that male Tyrannosaurs fought for dominance during the mating season by butting heads. The young, hatched from eggs, may have been about 3 feet long and 15 pounds in weight.

BODY CONSTRUCTION

Step 1.
Follow Steps 1 to 3 as per Camptosaurus for the Tyrannosaurus body (see figs T1 and T2).

Step 2.
Lay out the pattern for the lower jaw (see fig. T2). Cut the lower jaw section from the same piece of wood as the body and as close to the point where it will actually be attached as possible so as to achieve a greater consistency in the grain.

Step 3.
Cut out the lower jaw piece with a band saw.

Step 4.
Use a $^3/_8$-inch round-over bit to router the body, routering only those areas designated in the pattern (see fig. T2). Do not router around the bulge over the eyes, the area that will be inside the mouth, or the upper area beneath the neck. If you feel uncomfortable routering

---

REQUIRED MATERIALS

Body: One $14^1/_2$ x $3^1/_4$ x $^3/_4$-inch piece of stock
Mouth: Cut from scraps of above piece
Rear legs: Two 11 x $2^1/_2$ x $^3/_4$-inch pieces of stock
Arms: Two 2 x $1^1/_4$ x $^3/_8$-inch pieces of stock
Teeth and claws: 12 inches of $^1/_8$-inch-diameter dowel rod and 2 inches of $^3/_{16}$-inch-diameter dowel rod
Other: Two $^3/_8$-inch axle pegs for rear legs, and one $1^1/_8$-inch section of $^3/_{16}$-inch-diameter dowel rod for arms

---

very close to these points, stop short of them and trim or carve off the excess, and round in with a modeling knife. Do not router the lower jaw piece at this time.

Step 5.
With a $^3/_8$-inch bit, drill the rear leg hole at a 90-degree angle through the body.

Step 6.
With a $^3/_{16}$-inch bit, drill the front arm hole at a 90-degree angle through the body.

Step 7.
With a $^3/_{16}$-inch brad-point bit, at an angle of 90 degrees to the side of the body, drill the eye holes to a depth of $^3/_{32}$ inch (see figs. T2 and T3).

Step 8.
With a $^1/_8$-inch brad-point bit, at the center point of the round and at a 45-degree angle to the side of the body, drill the nostril holes to a depth of $^1/_8$ inch (see figs. T2 and T3).

Step 9.
Position the lower jaw in place at the requisite angle with the head, and see whether the contact areas meet well. There should be as little of a gap as possible between the two pieces. If it fits, proceed to the next step. If it does not fit, remove very small amounts at a time by carving, sanding, cutting, or rasping one or both of the contact points until a suitable joint is attained.

Step 10.
On the main body section, mark the positions for the teeth in the upper mouth (see fig. T3).

Step 11.
With a 1/8-inch brad-point bit, at an angle of 90 degrees to the line of the mouth, drill the teeth sockets to a depth of 1/8 inch.

Step 12.
Fine-sand the inside of the upper mouth.

Step 13.
From a 12-inch length of 1/8-inch-diameter dowel rod, make the upper teeth by fine-sanding the end of the dowel rod until nicely rounded.

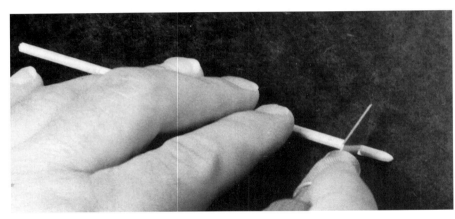

Then use a sharp modeling knife to cut the dowel to length. Repeat sanding and cutting until all ten teeth are done. The desired lengths, inclusive of the 1/8 inch that will go into the socket are as follows:
- First, third, and fourth pairs: 5/16 inch
- Second pair: 3/8 inch
- Fifth pair: 1/4 inch

Step 14.
Now use a pencil to mark the positions for the teeth in the lower jaw. (see fig. T3).

Step 15.
Hold the lower jaw in place with the upper and determine whether the positions of the lower teeth, as marked, will mesh with the upper. They should, but if not, adjust your markings accordingly, being careful not to place them too close to any of the edges.

Step 16.
When the lower teeth are properly aligned, use a 1/8-inch brad-point bit, at an angle of 90 degrees with the line of the mouth, to drill the sockets to a depth of 1/8 inch. *Do not* exceed this depth.

Step 17.
Now make the lower teeth, using the same procedure and dowel rod as for the upper. All lower teeth should be 1/4 inch long, inclusive of the length for each hole.

Step 18.
Fine-sand the inside of the lower jaw.

Step 19.
Using a toothpick, place a small amount of glue in each hole, and affix the upper and lower teeth in their appropriate positions.

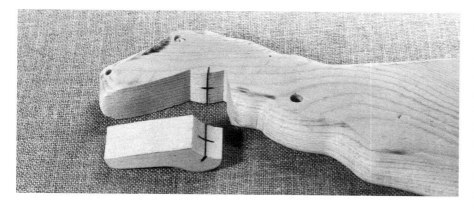

Step 20.
For the sake of structural soundness, necessary to successfully complete the model, the lower jaw must be pegged to the upper (see fig. T3). Without gluing, align the lower jaw with the upper and determine the center point of the contact area. Off this point with each piece, determine the lateral center points of the body and lower jaw widths.

◀ At the point on each piece where the two lines intersect, use a $^3/_{16}$-inch brad-point bit to drill holes to a depth of $^1/_8$ inch to $^3/_{16}$ inch at the angles shown in the figure.

Step 21.
Cut a $^3/_{16}$-inch-diameter dowel rod to a length equal to the total depth of both holes.
Step 22.
Glue the peg into the lower jaw.

◀ **Step 23.**
Glue the lower jaw to the upper jaw, and let it dry thoroughly.

Step 24.
Once dry, use a $^3/_8$-inch round-over bit to router the bottom edge of the lower jaw and the areas of the neck previously neglected.
Step 25.
Fine-sand the body.

REAR LEG CONSTRUCTION

The rear legs are made using Type A construction (see fig. T4). There are, however, several additional steps involved.

- Use a ³/₈-inch-diameter brad-point bit to drill the holes through the legs.
- Use a ³/₈-inch round-over bit to router the legs.

- When testing to see if the Tyrannosaurus balances on its rear legs, you should not have to remove any wood if the model tips backward. The addition of the rear claws on this and the two following models should take care of this problem.

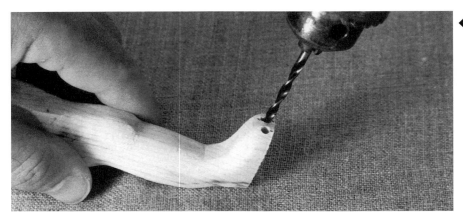

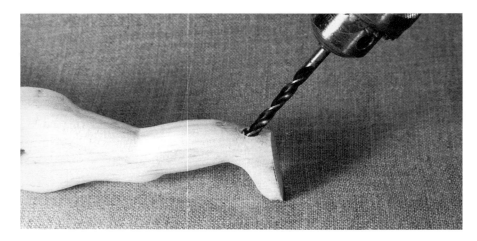

◄ **Step 1.**
Mark the holes for the three forward claws, and with a ¹/₈-inch brad-point bit, drill them at the angles designated in the figure to a depth of ¹/₈ inch.

Step 2.
From ¹/₈-inch-diameter dowel rod, make the claws in the same way you made the teeth. The central claw on each foot should be ³/₈ inch long, total, and each of the four outer claws should be ⁵/₁₆ inch long.

Step 3.
For the rear claw, mark the point for the hole, and with a ³/₁₆-inch brad-point bit, drill it at a 45-degree angle to a depth of ¹/₄ inch.

Step 4.
Fit a ³/₁₆-inch-diameter dowel rod into the rear hole, and cut it to a length that, when in position, will extend slightly beyond the bottom of the foot.

Step 5.
By sanding, taper and blunt the end of the rear claw to a length that, when in place, will extend to just touch whatever surface the dinosaur will stand on.

Step 6.
Fine-sand the areas where the various claws are to be glued.

Step 7.
Glue the claws in their proper positions using the same procedure described for the teeth.

Step 8.
Exclusive of the thickness of the head, cut the axle peg to a length of 1¹/₈ inches.

Step 9.
Finish and assemble as per basic Type A leg instructions.

ARM CONSTRUCTION

The arms are made using Type B construction in conjunction with the following additional steps and considerations (see fig. T5).

Step 1.
Use a $^3/_{16}$-inch-diameter brad-point bit to drill the holes in the arms.

Step 2.
Because these arms are so small, after cutting, do not attempt to router them. Instead, merely break the edges at the designated points by carving, sanding, or both.

◄ **Step 3.**
Mark the holes for the two claws, and with a $^1/_{16}$-inch bit, drill them at the designated angle to a depth of $^1/_8$ inch.

Step 4.
To make the claws, find the point at each end of two round toothpicks where the diameter increases to $^1/_{16}$ inch and mark.

Step 5.
From the points just marked, measure out toward the ends $^1/_4$ inch and use a modeling knife to cut off the tips.

Step 6.
By sanding, round off the new ends of the toothpicks.

Step 7.
With the modeling knife, at the point marked $^1/_4$ inch in, cut off the new ends of the toothpicks to obtain the claws.

Step 8.
Fine-sand the areas where the claws will be inserted.

Step 9.
Glue the claws in place using the same procedure described for teeth.

Step 10.
Cut the $^3/_{16}$-inch-diameter dowel rod for the arms to a length of $1^1/_8$ inches.

Step 11.
Continue as per basic Type B arm and leg construction.

FINISHING AND ASSEMBLY
Step 1.
Finish the body as desired.

Step 2.
Assemble as per basic Type A and B leg construction.

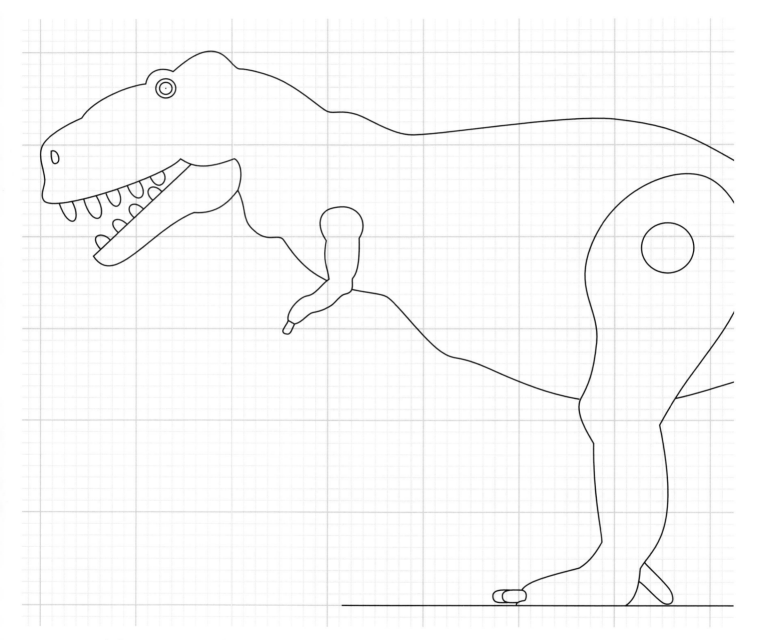

FIGURE T1. PLAN OF COMPLETED TYRANNOSAURUS (FULL-SCALE)

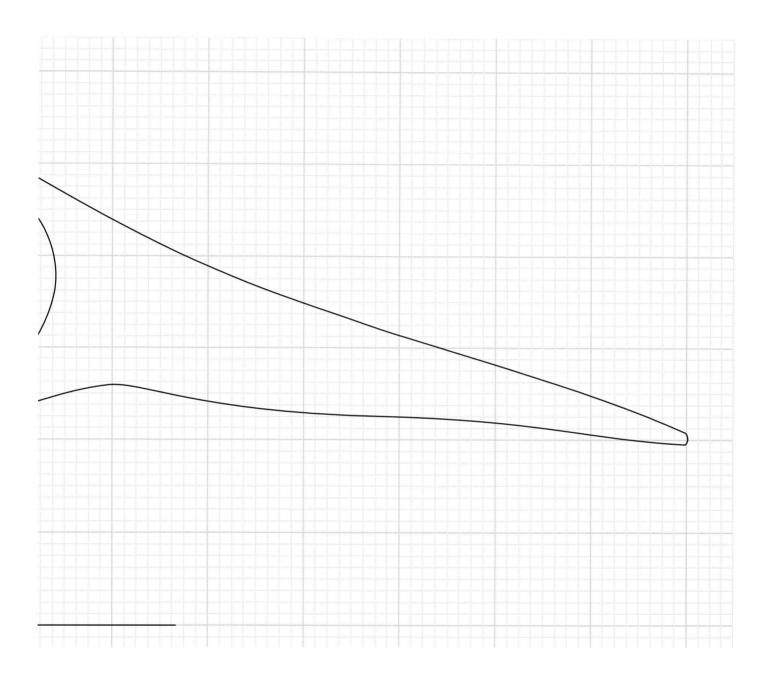

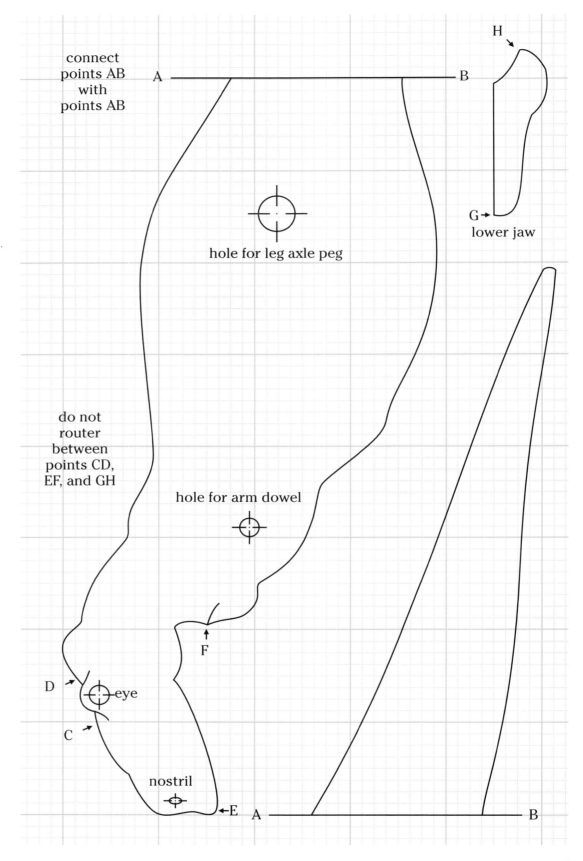

connect
points AB
with
points AB

A ——————— B

H

G→ lower jaw

hole for leg axle peg

do not
router
between
points CD,
EF, and GH

hole for arm dowel

F

D→
⊕—eye

C→

nostril

⊕

←E   A ——————— B

FIGURE T2. BODY AND LOWER JAW PATTERNS FOR TYRANNOSAURUS

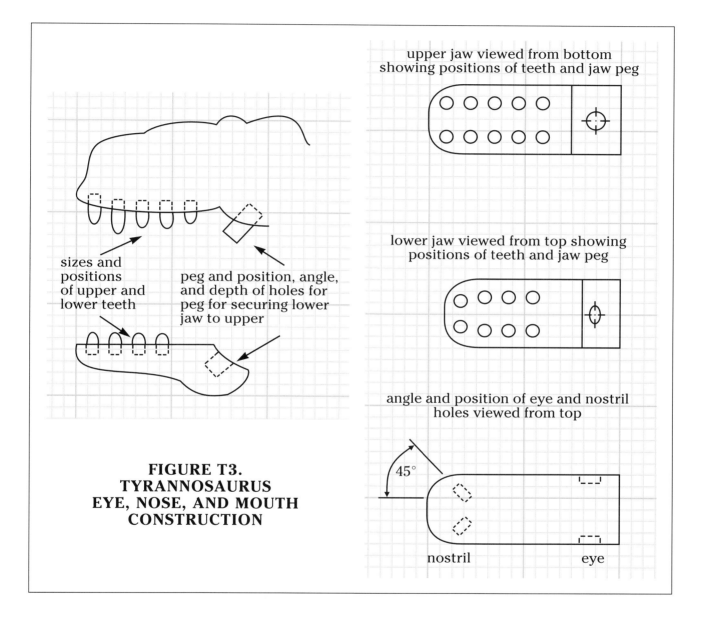

upper jaw viewed from bottom
showing positions of teeth and jaw peg

lower jaw viewed from top showing
positions of teeth and jaw peg

angle and position of eye and nostril
holes viewed from top

45°

nostril   eye

sizes and
positions
of upper and
lower teeth

peg and position, angle,
and depth of holes for
peg for securing lower
jaw to upper

**FIGURE T3.
TYRANNOSAURUS
EYE, NOSE, AND MOUTH
CONSTRUCTION**

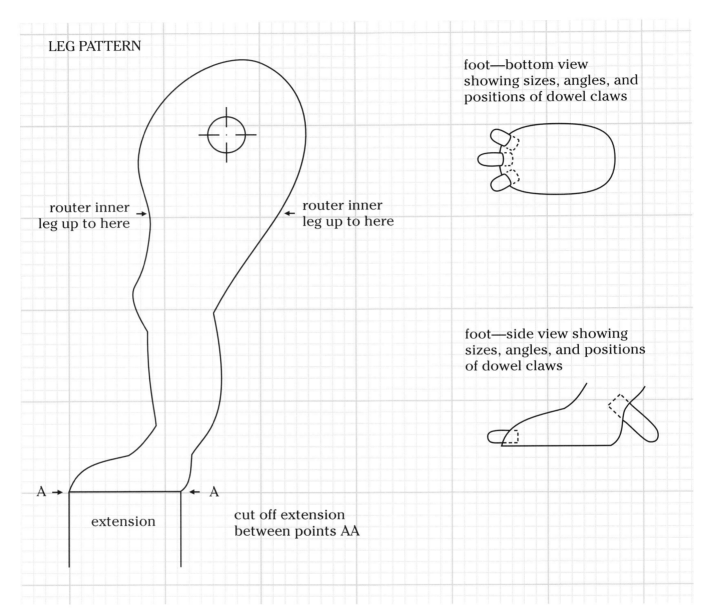

LEG PATTERN

router inner leg up to here

router inner leg up to here

A

A

extension

cut off extension between points AA

foot—bottom view showing sizes, angles, and positions of dowel claws

foot—side view showing sizes, angles, and positions of dowel claws

FIGURE T4. TYRANNOSAURUS REAR LEG PATTERN AND CONSTRUCTION

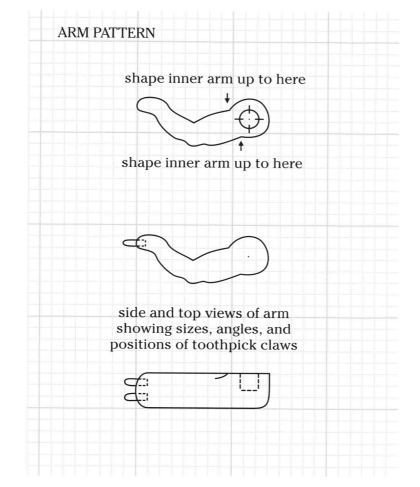

ARM PATTERN

shape inner arm up to here

shape inner arm up to here

side and top views of arm
showing sizes, angles, and
positions of toothpick claws

FIGURE T5. TYRANNOSAURUS ARM PATTERN AND CONSTRUCTION

Allosaurus

Allosaurus (Al-uh-SAWR-us): "Other, strange, or weird lizard"	or	**Antrodemus** (An-tro-DEE-mus): The original name
Class: Reptilia	or	Archosauria
Subclass or Infraclass: Dicipsida	or	Dinosauria
Superorder: Archosauria	or	Theropoda
Order: Saurischia	or	Avetheropoda
Suborder: Theropoda	or	Allosauria
Infraorder: Carnosauria		
Family: Allosauridae		Allosauridae
Subfamily:		Allosaurinae
Genus: *Allosaurus*		*Allosaurus*
Species: *Allosaurus fragilis*, *atrox*, and *amplexus*		*Allosaurus fragilis*, *atrox*, and *amplexus*

Close relatives: *Allosaurus fragilis*, *atrox*, and *amplexus* were all very similar. The main differences were in size, build, and head proportions. *Amplexus* was the largest, and *fragilis* the smallest. *Fragilis* had a shorter and taller skull and more pointed preorbital horns.

Length: 30 to 45 feet (10 to 15 meters)*

Height: 9 to 12 feet at the hip (3 to 4 meters)*

Weight: 2 to 6 tons (up to 5.4 metric tons)*

*Note: The length, height, and weight specifications cover the range for adults of the three species of Allosaurs.

O thniel Marsh made the first discoveries of these best-known and largest of the Late Jurassic predators. *Allosaurus fragilis* was found in 1877, and *A. atrox* and *A. amplexus* were uncovered a year later. All come from Morrison Formation sites such as Como Bluffs and are found in Montana, Wyoming, South Dakota, Colorado, and Utah. In 1927, a spectacular find was made at the Cleveland-Lloyd Quarry, Utah. There, the fossilized skeletons of forty-four Allosaurs were unearthed. Since, the same site

has yielded another sixteen to twenty-six sets of remains. Despite the relatively early discovery of Allosaurus, it was not officially described until the 1920s, when C. W. Gilmore undertook the task. Some authorities suggest that some Allosaurs may have survived into the early Cretaceous period.

As with other carnivorous dinosaurs, there is debate among the scientific community over whether Allosaurs were cold- or warm-blooded. The proponents for a cold-blooded metabolism argue that prey such as Sauropods were too big for even a pack of slow, clumsy Allosaurs to attack and kill. They also believe the predator-to-prey ratio was too high for the ecosystem to support Allosaurs if they were warm-blooded, and they must have been scavengers. Some cold-blooded supporters do, however, concede that the smaller juveniles may have been more active than adults. Countering these arguments, the warm-blooded enthusiasts maintain that Allosaurs were speedy, agile, active hunters.

For its size, Allosaurus possessed a very graceful body that was supported in a horizontal position by two powerful hind legs. As with other bipedal dinosaurs, the powerful, stiffened tail, constituting half the beast's length, acted as a counterbalance for the torso. Each hind foot sported three forward-facing toes with claws. A fourth toe with claw extended to the rear. On these legs, it has been estimated that Allosaurs could walk at a rate of 5 miles per hour. At a trot, their stride was about 9 feet. Still, even warm-blooded supporters feel that the legs were structured in such a manner that Allosaurs were not as speedy as the later Tyrannosaurs. It was once be-

lieved that Allosaurs hopped about on their legs like kangaroos, but this idea is no longer supported. It is, however, believed that these animals were powerful swimmers.

From the shoulders, there were two arms. Some authorities maintain that these appendages were not very functional. Others uphold that they were quite powerful and, with three well-developed clawed fingers capable of grasping, the arms were very useful when grappling with prey. Whatever the case, Allosaurus arms and hands were certainly more functional than those of Tyrannosaurs.

Supported on a powerful arched, flexible neck was a large skull about 3 feet long. The massive jaws contained curved, serrated teeth between 2 and 4 inches long. The jaws were jointed, making them flexible and expandable. As such, they were suitable for gulping down large chunks of meat. Of interest is the fact that Allosaur eyes were twice as large as those of any other carnivorous dinosaur. Above and slightly in front of the eyes were two horn ridges. It is believed these were used for butting heads.

Although it is probable that Allosaurs laid eggs, there has been some suggestion that they gave live birth. Babies may have been about 20 inches long, and perhaps the parents fed and protected them. The remains of juveniles have been found, indicating they were about 10 feet long and stood about 3 1/2 feet tall at the hip.

In terms of social organization, Allosaurs probably lived in packs or at least pairs. In such an organization, they hunted for Apatosaurs and Stegosaurs. They shared the hunting grounds with Ceratosaurus.

REQUIRED MATERIALS

Body: One 14 x 3 x 3/4-inch piece of stock
Lower jaw: One 1 1/2 x 1/2 x 3/4-inch piece of stock
Legs: Two 8 1/4 x 2 x 3/4-inch pieces of stock
Arms: Two 6 3/4 x 1 x 3/4-inch pieces of stock
Teeth and claws: 10 inches of 1/8-inch-diameter dowel rod
Jaw socket support: 3/8-inch of 3/16-inch-diameter dowel rod
Other: Two 1/4-inch-diameter axle pegs for the arms, and two
  3/8-inch-diameter axle pegs for the legs

BODY CONSTRUCTION

The Allosaurus body (figs. A1 and A2) is made using the same procedures described for Tyrannosaurus, except as noted below.

Step 1.

Use a 3/8-inch round-over bit to router the body, routering the designated areas only. Do not router the area on the top of the head from the base of the skull to the tip of the nose. Also, do not router edges of the upper jaw. (see figs. A1 and A2).

Step 2.
Use a $3/8$-inch-diameter brad-point bit to drill the rear leg hole at a 90-degree angle through the body.

Step 3.
Use a $1/4$-inch-diameter brad-point bit to drill the front arm hole at a 90-degree angle through the body.

Step 4.
Use a $1/4$-inch chamfer bit set to cut to a depth of $3/16$ inch to router the area from just in front of the eyes to the tip of the nose.

Step 5.
Use a $3/16$-inch-diameter brad-point bit to drill the eye holes $1/16$-inch deep at a 90-degree angle to the side of the head (see figs. A2 and A3).

Step 6.
Use a $1/8$-inch-diameter brad-point bit to drill the nostril holes $1/8$ inch deep at a 90-degree angle to the surface of the chamfer (see figs. A2 and A3).

Step 7.
Use a $1/8$-inch brad-point bit to drill all tooth holes to a depth of $1/8$ inch in the upper and lower jaws (see fig. A3).

Step 8.
All teeth are made from $1/8$-inch-diameter dowel rod. Inclusive of the $1/8$ inch that will fit into the holes in the jaws, the lengths of the teeth are as follows:

Upper teeth, from the front:

First, third, fourth, and fifth pairs: $1/4$ inch
Second pair: $5/16$ inch
Lower teeth, from the front:
First and second pairs: $1/4$ inch
Third and fourth pairs: $3/16$ inch

Step 9.
Use a $3/8$-inch length of $3/16$-inch-diameter dowel rod to secure the lower jaw to the upper (see fig. A3).

LEG CONSTRUCTION
The rear legs are made using Type A construction (see fig. A4). There are, however, several additional steps involved to create the claws.

- Use a $3/8$-inch-diameter brad-point bit to drill the hole at a 90-degree angle through the legs.
- Router the designated areas with a $3/8$-inch round-over bit.

Step 1.
Use a $1/8$-inch-diameter brad-point bit to drill all holes for claws at the designated angles to a depth of $1/8$ inch.

Step 2.
All claws on the rear legs are made from $1/8$-inch-diameter dowel rod. The four outer claws should be $5/16$ inch long and the two inner claws $3/8$ inch long, inclusive of the portion that will fit into the holes. The exact length of each of the rear claws needs to be determined during the course of construction, as in Steps 7 and 8 of Type A construction or in 4 and 5 of Tyrannosaurus leg construction.

Step 3.
Exclusive of the thickness of the head, cut each $3/8$-inch-diameter axle peg to a length of $1\,1/8$ inches.

ARM CONSTRUCTION
The arms are also made using the Type A construction method (see fig. A5). There are, however, several additional procedures required to create the claws.

Step 1.
Use a $1/4$-inch-diameter brad-point bit to drill the hole at a 90-degree angle through the arm. Router the designated areas with a $3/8$-inch round-over bit.

Step 2.
Use a $1/8$-inch-diameter brad-point bit to drill all holes for claws at the designated angles to a depth of $1/8$ inch.

Step 3.
All claws on the hands are made from $1/8$-inch-diameter dowel rod. The four outer claws should be $1/4$ inch long and the two inner claws $5/16$ inch long, inclusive of the portion that will fit into the holes.

Step 4.
Exclusive of the thickness of the head, cut each $1/4$-inch-diameter axle peg to a length of $1\,1/8$ inches.

FINISHING AND ASSEMBLY
Step 1.
Finish the body as desired.
Step 2.
Assemble as per basic Type A and B leg construction.

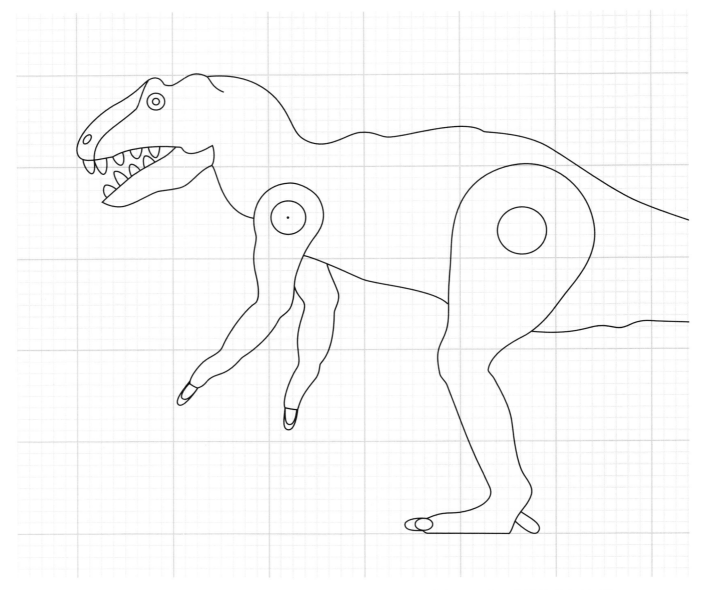

FIGURE A1. PLAN OF COMPLETED ALLOSAURUS (FULL-SCALE)

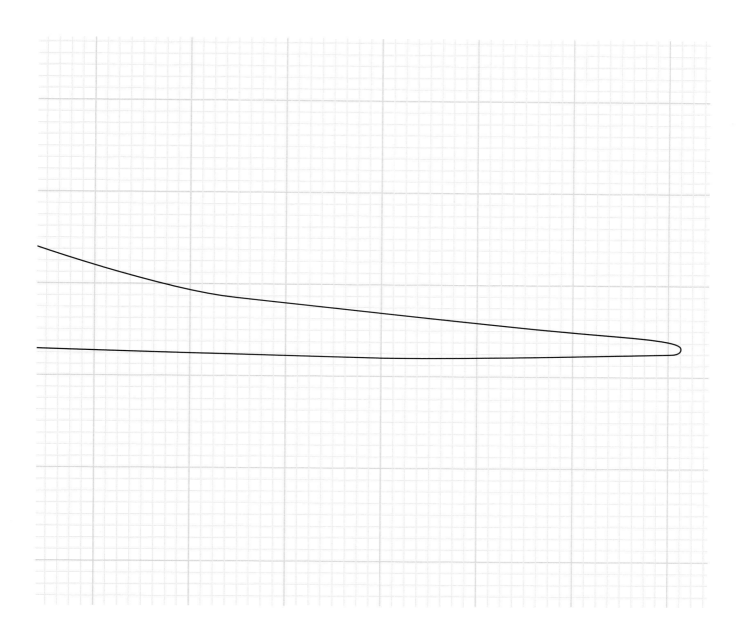

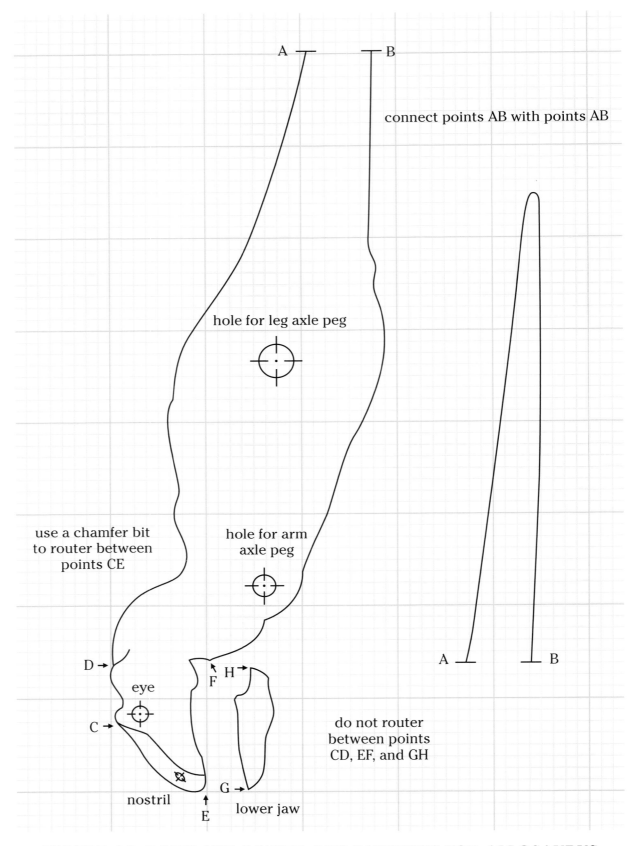

connect points AB with points AB

hole for leg axle peg

use a chamfer bit
to router between
points CE

hole for arm
axle peg

D →

eye

C →

H →
F

do not router
between points
CD, EF, and GH

nostril
E

G →

lower jaw

A

B

FIGURE A2. BODY AND LOWER JAW PATTERNS FOR ALLOSAURUS

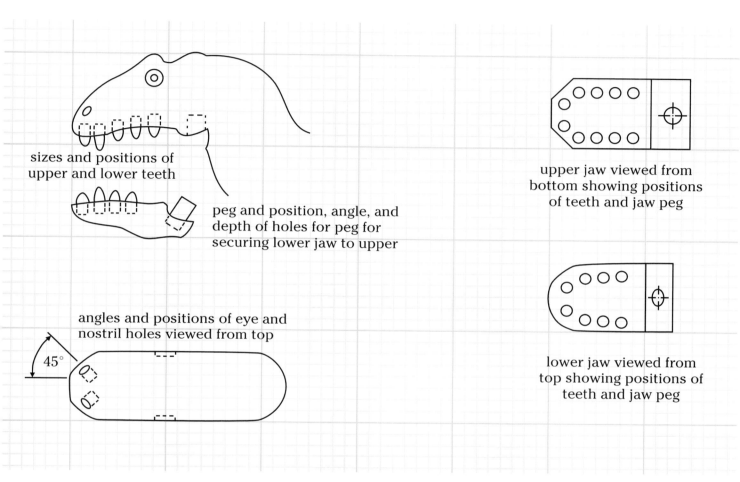

sizes and positions of
upper and lower teeth

peg and position, angle, and
depth of holes for peg for
securing lower jaw to upper

angles and positions of eye and
nostril holes viewed from top

45°

upper jaw viewed from
bottom showing positions
of teeth and jaw peg

lower jaw viewed from
top showing positions of
teeth and jaw peg

FIGURE A3. ALLOSAURUS EYE, NOSE, AND MOUTH CONSTRUCTION

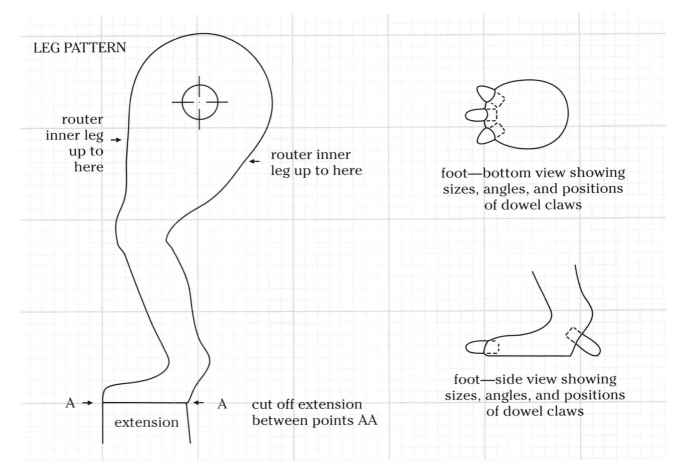

FIGURE A4. ALLOSAURUS REAR LEG PATTERN AND CONSTRUCTION

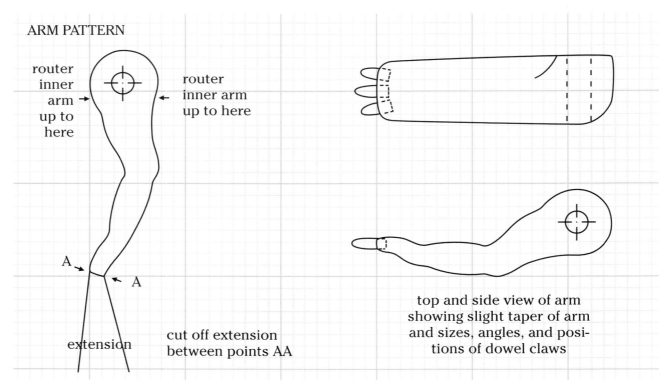

FIGURE A5. ALLOSAURUS ARM PATTERN AND CONSTRUCTION

Ceratosaurus nasicornis

Ceratosaurus (sair-AT-o-sawr-us): "Horned lizard"

Class: Reptilia	or	Archosauria
Subclass: Diapsida	or	Dinosauria
Superorder: Archosauria	or	Theropoda
Order: Saurischia	or	Paleotheropoda
Suborder: Theropoda	or	Ceratosauria
Infraorder: Carnosauria		
Family: Ceratosauridae		Ceratosauridae
Genus: *Ceratosaurus*		*Ceratosaurus*
Species: *Ceratosaurus nasicornis*		*Ceratosaurus nasicornis*

Close relatives: *Ceratosaurus ingens*
Length: 18.5 feet (5.64 meters) with indications of up to 30 feet (9.14 meters)
Height: 4.95 feet (1.51 meters) at 18.5 feet long
Weight: 1,150 pounds (524 kilograms)

*C*eratosaurus nasicornis* was first described by its discoverer, Othniel Marsh, in 1894. Its remains are found in the Late Jurassic Morrison Formation of Colorado and Wyoming. While some authorities class this animal in the family Megalosauridae, most accord it its own family group.

Ceratosaurus was a midsized meateater, smaller than its contemporary Allosaurus, with which it shared the terrain. Like all Carnosaurs, it was bipedal, moving about on its long, powerful hind legs. The forearms, while robust and strong, were much shorter. On the rear feet, there were three long,

forward-pointing toes and the reduced rearward pointing one typical of Theropods. The hands each had four fingers. All digits displayed long, sharp claws. When moving, Ceratosaurus's muscular tail was held straight out behind to act as a counterbalance for the rest of the body.

This dinosaur's most noticeable features—those for which it was named—were the single short horn at the end of its snout and two smaller horny bumps over the eyes. The skull was of a fairly light structure, but the jaws were very powerful. Some authorities believe that the jaws of the Ceratosaurus had flexible areas that allowed them to expand to accept relatively larger chunks of meat while eating. The teeth were saberlike and serrated. The upper ones were considerably longer than the lower. Down the neck and back to the end of the tail was a row of bony platelike scutes over the spines of the vertebrae. Ceratosaurus was the only carnosaur to possess such "armor," and although it was not the basis for its name, these scutes really did make the animal appear serrated.

Its medium size in association with its powerful legs indicates that Ceratosaurus was an active hunter. There is seemingly a general acceptance of this fact by the proponents of both cold- and warm-bloodedness. For predatory activities, these fast, nimble hunters moved about the floodplains and shorelines in packs, searching for prey ranging from the defenseless Camptosaurus to the mighty Apatosaurus.

Ceratosaurus's horn was not actively employed as a killing weapon. Instead, it probably served as a butting device in disputes with rival males during mating season. It has even been suggested that only the males had horns. For real hunting and fighting, Ceratosaurus relied on its teeth and claws. At least one authority believes the beast may actually have been able to bounce on its tail while kicking out and clawing with its hind feet and hands. Another scientist maintains that Ceratosaurus was quite possibly at home in the water, where it used its deep, laterally flattened tail as a scull to propel it along. Ceratosaurus was truly an animal to be reckoned with as it roamed the Late Jurassic landscape in search of food.

REQUIRED MATERIALS

Body: One 7$\frac{1}{2}$ x 2$\frac{1}{4}$ x $\frac{1}{2}$-inch piece of stock, plus enough extra to leave a 4-inch extension off the tail

Legs: Two 7$\frac{1}{2}$ x 1$\frac{3}{8}$ x $\frac{1}{2}$-inch pieces of stock

Arms: Two 1$\frac{3}{8}$ x $\frac{1}{2}$ x $\frac{3}{8}$-inch pieces of stock

Spines: One 12-inch length of $\frac{1}{8}$-inch-diameter dowel rod

Horn: One $\frac{1}{2}$-inch length of $\frac{3}{16}$-inch-diameter dowel rod

Teeth and claws: At least nine round toothpicks

Other: Two $\frac{1}{4}$-inch-diameter axle pegs for the legs, and one 1-inch length of $\frac{1}{8}$-inch-diameter dowel rod for the arms

BODY CONSTRUCTION
Step 1.
Follow Steps 1 to 3 as per Camptosaurus and Tyrannosaurus, but leave extra wood for an extension off the end of the tail (see figs. CR1 and CR2).
Step 2.
Use a $\frac{1}{4}$-inch round-over bit to router the body, routering only those areas designated in the pattern (see fig. CR2). Do not router the area from behind the bulge over the eyes to the end of the nose, the area along the edge of the mouth, or the region beneath the neck. Do not router the lower jaw piece at this time.

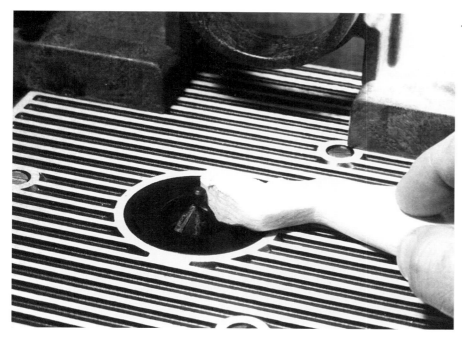

Step 3.
With a ¼-inch chamfer bit set to a ⅛-inch cutting depth, router the area from just in front of the eye bulge to the tip of the nose.

Step 4.
With a ¼-inch brad-point bit, drill the rear leg hole at a 90-degree angle through the body.

Step 5.
With a ⅛-inch brad-point bit, drill the arm hole at a 90-degree angle completely through the body.

Step 6.
With a ⅛-inch brad-point bit, perpendicular to the side of the body, drill the eye holes to a depth of 1/16 inch (see figs. CR2 and CR3).

Step 7.
With a 1/16-inch bit, at a 90-degree angle to the face of the chamfer, drill the nostril holes to a depth of 1/16 inch (see figs. CR2 and CR3).

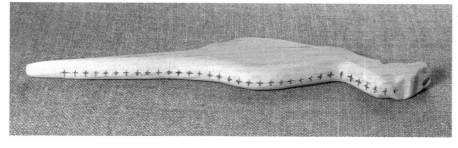

Step 8.
Use a pencil to mark the thirty-five points down the centerline of the back for the holes for the spines (see fig. CR4).

Step 9.
Once it is ascertained that the positioning is correct, re-mark the points with a sharp awl.

Step 10.
With a ⅛-inch brad-point bit, drill each of the thirty-five holes to a depth of ⅛ inch at a 90-degree angle to each particular point (see fig. CR4).

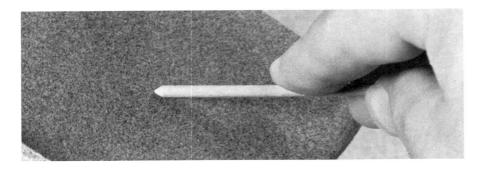

Step 11.
Take the 12-inch length of ⅛-inch-diameter dowel rod, and by sanding, shape ⅛ inch at each end to a moderate point (see fig. CR4).

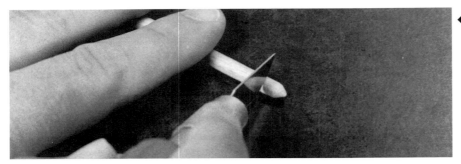

◀ **Step 12.**
With a modeling knife, cut off a ¼-inch length from each end.

Step 13.
Repeat Steps 11 and 12 until sixteen ¼-inch pieces have been cut.
Step 14.
Now repeat Steps 11 and 12, but tapering only ¹⁄₁₆ inch of the dowel ends, and cut off ³⁄₁₆-inch lengths to make the remaining nineteen spines.
Step 15.
Place these small pieces in separate envelopes according to size and put aside.

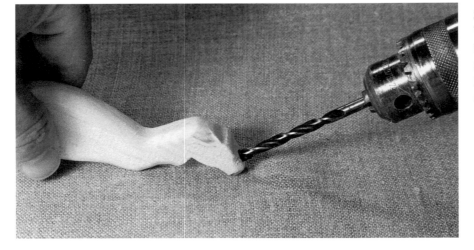

Step 16.
With a ³⁄₁₆-inch brad-point bit, at a 90-degree angle to the top of the nose, drill the hole for the nasal horn to a depth of ⅛ inch (see fig. CR3).

Step 17.
Take the small section of $^3/_{16}$-inch-diameter dowel rod, and by sanding, shape $^1/_8$ inch on one end to a modest point for the nasal horn (see figs. CR1 and CR3).

Step 18.
With a modeling knife, cut off a $^1/_4$-inch length of the dowel, inclusive of the shaped portion, to make the horn. Put it aside until later assembly.

Step 19.
Check the alignment and joint of the lower jaw with the upper, and alter as necessary as per Step 9 of the Tyrannosaurus body construction section.

Step 20.
On the main body section, mark the positions for the teeth on the upper mouth (see fig. CR3).

Step 21.
With a $^1/_{16}$-inch bit, at an angle of 90 degrees to the line of the mouth, drill the six upper tooth sockets to depths of $^1/_{16}$ inch.

Step 22.
Make the upper and lower teeth as follows from round toothpicks. First find the point at each end of five toothpicks where the diameter increases to $^1/_{16}$ inch and mark. With a modeling knife, $^1/_8$ inch out from the points marked on four toothpicks and $^5/_{32}$ inch out on the ends of the other, cut off the ends. By sanding, shape each new end to a point, being careful not to reduce

the length. Now use a modeling knife to cut off the ends at the point initially marked to create the teeth.

Step 23.
With a pencil, mark the positions for the teeth on the lower jaw (see fig. CR3).

Step 24.
Hold the lower jaw in place with the upper and determine whether the positions of the lower teeth, as marked, will mesh with the upper. They should, but if not, adjust your markings accordingly, being careful not to place them too close to any of the edges.

Step 25.
When the lower teeth are properly aligned, use a $^1/_{16}$-inch bit, at an angle of 90 degrees to the line of the mouth, to drill the sockets to depths of $^1/_{16}$ inch. Be extremely careful not to exceed this depth.

Step 26.
Sand the inside of the upper and lower jaws to a fine finish.

Step 27.
Using a pin, place a small amount of glue in each hole, and affix the upper and lower teeth in their appropriate places. The longer teeth form the second pair back on the top. Do not get any glue on what will be exposed surfaces.

Step 28.
For the sake of structural soundness, the lower jaw needs to be pegged to the upper. Follow the procedure outlined in Step 20 for Tyrannosaurus, but use a $^1/_8$-inch brad-point bit to drill the holes in the upper and lower jaws to a depth of $^1/_8$ inch (see fig. CR3).

Step 29.
Cut a $^1/_4$-inch length from a $^1/_8$-inch-diameter dowel rod.

Step 30.
Assemble the lower jaw as per Steps 22 and 23 for Tyrannosaurus.

Step 31.
Once dry, use a $^1/_4$-inch round-over bit to router the bottom edge of

the lower jaw and the areas of the neck previously neglected.

Step 32.

Fine-sand the rest of the body.

Step 33.

With a toothpick or pin, place a small amount of glue in the hole on the nose and insert the nasal horn.

Step 34.

With a toothpick or pin, place a small amount of glue in the sixth through the twenty-first holes from the head and affix the $1/4$-inch spines.

Step 35.

Put glue in the remaining holes and affix the $3/16$-inch spines.

LEG CONSTRUCTION

The legs are made using the Type A construction method (see fig. CR5). There are, however, several additional procedures required to create the claws.

- Use a $1/4$-inch brad-point bit to drill the hole through the legs for the axle pegs.
- Use a $1/4$-inch round-over bit to router the areas desig-nated (see fig. CR5).

Step 1.

Mark the holes for the three for-ward claws on each foot, and with a $1/16$-inch bit, drill them at the angles designated (see fig. CR5) to depths of $1/8$ inch.

Step 2.

For the rear claw, mark the points for the holes, and with a $1/16$-inch bit, at a 45-degree angle, drill each $1/8$ inch deep.

Step 3.

From three round toothpicks, make the six forward claws in the same way you made the teeth. They should be $1/16$ inch in diame-ter at the base and $5/16$ inch in length.

Step 4.

Make the two rear claws from one round toothpick. Find the point at each end of the toothpick where the diameter increases to $1/16$ inch, mark, and cut off. Fit the thicker ends of the two pieces into the holes, and cut them to lengths that extend slightly beyond the bot-toms of the feet. By sanding, taper and blunt the exposed ends of the rear claws to lengths that, when in place, will just touch whatever sur-face the dinosaur will stand on.

Step 5.

Fine-sand the areas where the vari-ous claws will be glued.

Step 6.

Glue the claws into place, using the same procedure described for teeth.

Step 7.

Exclusive of the thickness of the head, cut each axle peg to a length of $3/4$ inch.

Step 8.

Proceed as per basic Type A leg instructions.

ARM CONSTRUCTION

The arms are made using the Type B construction method, (see fig. CR5). *Do not* attempt to router these; they are too small.

Step 1.

To accommodate the dowel rod, use a $1/8$-inch brad-point bit to drill a hole $1/8$ inch deep on the inside of each arm.

Step 2.

Mark, cut, taper the hands, and break the edges in the same man-ner done with Ornithomimus and Pachycephalosaurus.

Step 3.

Cut a $7/8$-inch length of $1/8$-inch-diameter dowel rod.

Step 4.

Proceed as per basic Type B con-struction.

FINISHING AND ASSEMBLY

Step 1.

Finish as desired.

Step 2.

Assemble as per basic Type A and B arm and leg construction.

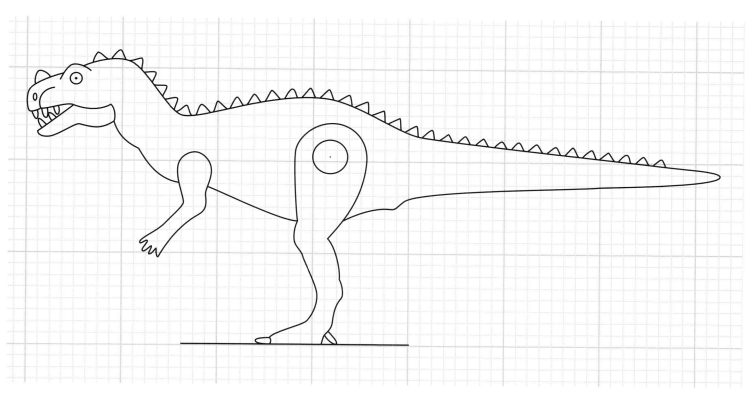

FIGURE CR1. PLAN OF COMPLETED CERATOSAURUS (FULL-SCALE)

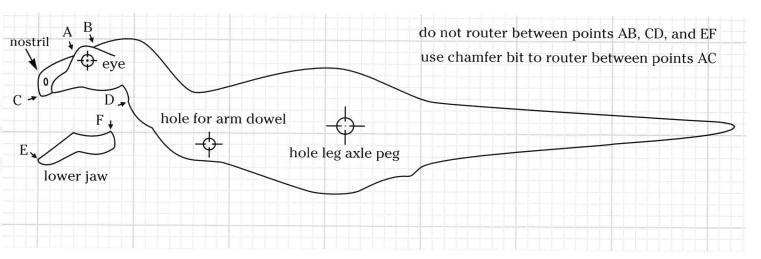

FIGURE CR2. BODY AND LOWER JAW PATTERNS FOR CERATOSAURUS

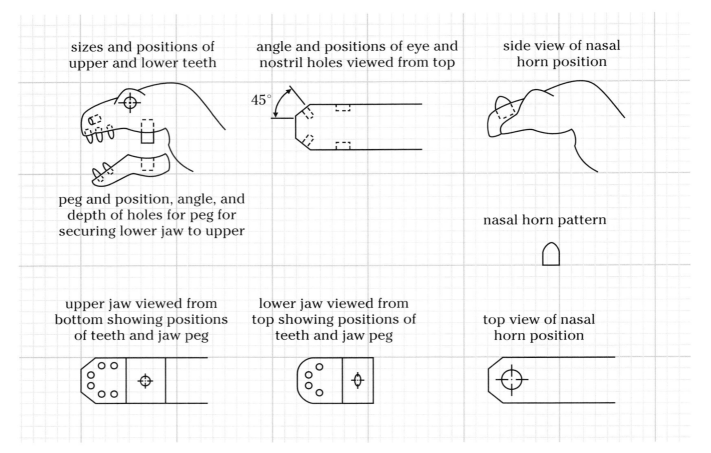

sizes and positions of
upper and lower teeth

angle and positions of eye and
nostril holes viewed from top

side view of nasal
horn position

45°

peg and position, angle, and
depth of holes for peg for
securing lower jaw to upper

nasal horn pattern

upper jaw viewed from
bottom showing positions
of teeth and jaw peg

lower jaw viewed from
top showing positions of
teeth and jaw peg

top view of nasal
horn position

FIGURE CR3. CERATOSAURUS EYE, NOSE, AND MOUTH CONSTRUCTION

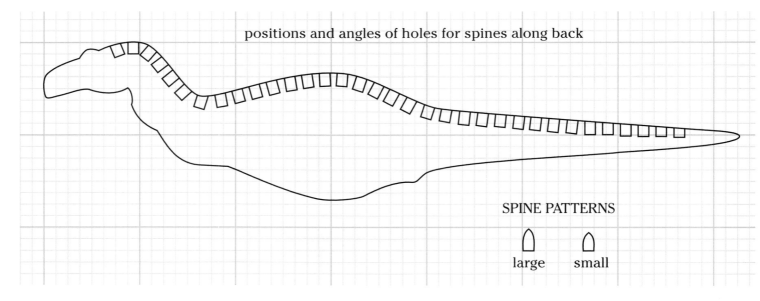

positions and angles of holes for spines along back

SPINE PATTERNS

large   small

FIGURE CR4. CERATOSAURUS SPINE PATTERNS AND CONSTRUCTION

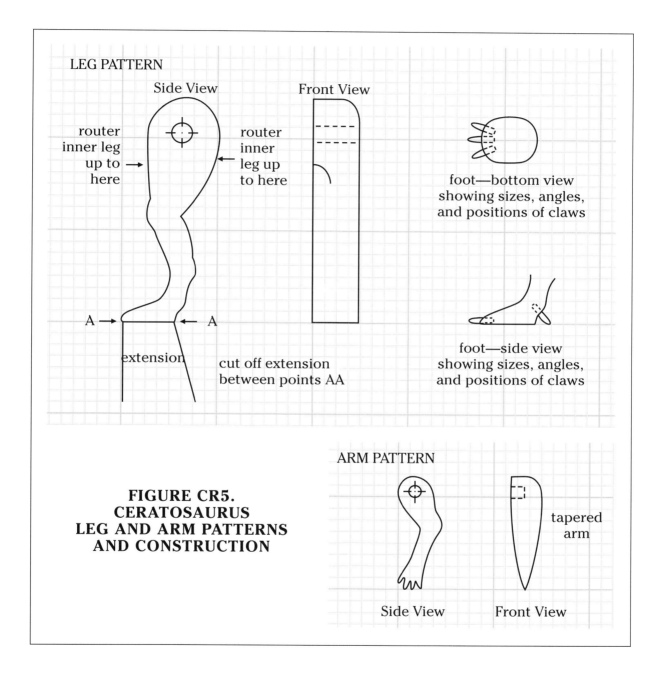

LEG PATTERN

Side View

Front View

router inner leg up to here →

← router inner leg up to here

A → ← A

extension

cut off extension between points AA

foot—bottom view showing sizes, angles, and positions of claws

foot—side view showing sizes, angles, and positions of claws

FIGURE CR5. CERATOSAURUS LEG AND ARM PATTERNS AND CONSTRUCTION

ARM PATTERN

tapered arm

Side View

Front View

Monoclonius nasicornis

Monoclonius (mon-o-CLONE-ee-us): "One horned"
Order: Ornithischia
Suborder: Ceratopsia
Infraorder: Thyreophora (Ceratopsia)
Family: Ceratopsidae
Genus: *Monoclonius*
Species: *Monoclonius nasicornis*

Close relatives: Brachyceratops,
Pachyrhinosaurus, and Styracosaurus
Length: 15 to 20 feet (4.5 to 6 meters)
Weight: 2.5 to 3 tons (2.25 to 2.7 metric tons)

Monoclonius nasicornis, like its relative Triceratops, was a member of the family Ceratopsidae, meaning "horned face." Its remains come from the Late Cretaceous Oldman Formation, Red Deer River, Alberta, Canada. Those of its very close relative *Monoclonius cassus* are found in the Judith River Formation of Montana. Centrosaurs and Eoceratops are two more genera of the same family that were quite similar to Monoclonius. In fact, some authorities feel they are really the same animal. Another creature, 6-foot-long Brachyceratops, is felt by some to merely be a baby Monoclonius. Whatever the case, Monoclonius itself was one of the first true Ceratopsids to evolve in what is now North America.

Monoclonius and all other Ceratopsids were quadrupeds. It is believed, however, that they evolved from bipedal ancestors. The front legs of Monoclonius dinosaurs were noticeably shorter than their rear legs, and one of the main controversies surrounding these creatures centers on them. Traditionally, the forelimbs are represented flexed, with the "elbow" out to the side like a modern lizard. More recent opinion maintains that as with other dinosaurs, the front legs were positioned directly beneath the body. All four feet were short and broad. Those in front had four toes with hooflike claws on each. Five toes with the same type of claws were on the rear feet.

The nature of the legs and the bulk of the body naturally lead to questions about speed. Traditionally, the viewpoint has been that Ceratopsids, like other dinosaurs, were cold-blooded and, therefore, slow, ponderous beasts. Proponents of this idea are often the same as those who maintain the front legs were flexed out to the sides, and they use this belief to support their opinion. They also uphold that the main leg bones, front and rear, could not stand the shock and stress of fast movement; they would have shattered. On the other hand, there are currently a number of authorities who feel that, in fact, these dinosaurs were quite fast and agile. These are the individuals who say the legs were positioned straight, beneath the torso. They also state the bone structure was capable of handling the stress of rapid movement. Ceratopsians such as Monoclonius are compared to modern rhinoceroses, and consequently, it is thought that they could gallop, perhaps as fast as 30 miles per hour.

The tails were relatively short and stubby, but there is debate over how they were carried. Some authorities believe they were carried low; others maintain they were held straight out behind One noted scientist has pointed out that there was a crisscross of stiffening rods throughout the tail. So however it was carried, it was not very flexible.

Characteristic of all Ceratopsids was the huge head, which displayed a number of interesting features. The mouth possessed a sharp, parrotlike beak, used to snip off tough, fibrous vegetation like twigs and leaves of low-growing cycads and palm trees for food. With a scissorslike action, sharp upper and lower teeth along the sides of the mouth meshed to slice these morsels into smaller pieces. As the teeth wore out, they were continually replaced with new ones. During the chewing process, the food was held in place and controlled by cheek pouches. All of this seems to have suitably prepared coarse vegetation for digestion. There is no evidence that these animals had gizzard stones like some dinosaurs that will be discussed later.

The large jaws housing the beak and teeth required powerful muscles to operate them and deal with the tough food. It was primarily for the attachment of these muscles and those supporting the huge head that the neck frills existed. While undoubtedly the frills also served as protective devices, this was a secondary function. Additionally, some authorities believe they could be used to intimidate opponents, either rivals in the same group or predatory enemies. When viewed from the front, a Ceratopsid with its head lowered and its frill up would create the illusion of being considerably larger than it actually was.

All Ceratopsids are categorized in one of two groups, depending on whether they possessed long or short frills. Generally, the animals with long frills had a pair of long brow horns, one over each eye, and a single short horn on the nose. The short-frilled versions, of which Monoclonius was one, basically showed the reverse, with a single long nasal horn and, at best, mere bumps hinting at horns over the eyes. The well-known Triceratops was the exception to the rule, having long brow horns in association with a short frill.

As a short-frilled form, Monoclonius possessed the typical long, upward-pointing nasal horn and pair of short bumps over the eyes. A long, spikelike protrusion was found at the bottom of the frill on either side. The bone inside the frill was not a solid sheet, but the frill had openings in it that helped reduce the weight. These were covered over with skin, however, creating the illusion that the frill was solid.

The purpose of the facial horns is debated, despite their seemingly obvious function. Some scientists maintain they were not used for defense against enemies, but only in contests between rival males. Opponents of this theory counter with the fact that the females had horns, too. Also, they point out that these protrusions were too developed for a special function requiring them to be extremely sharp and, as such, too lethal to be employed between rivals of the same species. The ease with which Monoclonius could use its highly flexible head with vertically pointing horn to come up beneath the soft, unprotected stomach of a predator has been demonstrated.

The young were hatched from eggs laid in nests. Because the teeth and beaks of the juveniles were weak, it is quite probable they received parental care. Without the ability to chew, and lacking gizzard stones, youngsters may have been fed regurgitated prechewed food by their parents. The youngsters were also born with undeveloped neck frills, and they lacked horns.

Ceratopsids are frequently compared with modern rhinos because of their powerful bulk and horns. In terms of their lifestyle and place in the ecosystem, however, they were probably the Late Cretaceous equivalent of buffalo. Roaming around in herds, they browsed on low-growing vegetation in open and semiopen upland terrain. When threatened by enemies, they may have gone into a formation similar to that of modern musk oxen. Basically, the adults may have formed a ring around the young, with heads facing out, presenting a dense, deadly hedgerow of spikes to ward off attackers.

REQUIRED MATERIALS

Body: One 7 x 2^1/$_2$ x ^{3}/$_4$-inch piece of stock
Rear legs: Two 7^1/$_2$ x 1^1/$_4$ x ^{3}/$_4$-inch pieces of stock
Front legs: Two 6^1/$_2$ x 1 x ^{1}/$_2$-inch pieces of stock
Frill: One 2 x 1^1/$_2$ x ^{3}/$_4$-inch piece of stock
Horns: 2^1/$_2$ inches of ^{1}/$_4$-inch-diameter dowel rod
Other: Two ^{3}/$_8$-inch-diameter axle pegs for the rear legs, and two ^{1}/$_4$-inch-diameter axle pegs for the front legs

---

BODY CONSTRUCTION
Step 1.
Follow Steps 1 to 3 as per Camptosaurus (see figs. M1 and M2).

Monoclonius body showing routered and unroutered areas

Step 2.
Use a ^{3}/$_8$-inch round-over bit to router the body, routering only the areas designated in the pattern (see fig. M2). Do not router the area from just in front of the bulge over the eyes back through the location the neck frill will fit over.

Step 3.
With a ^{3}/$_8$-inch-diameter brad-point bit, drill the rear leg hole through the body.

Step 4.
With a ^{1}/$_4$-inch brad-point bit, drill the front leg holes through the body.

Step 5.
With a ^{3}/$_{16}$-inch brad-point bit, perpendicular to the side of the body, drill the eye holes to a depth of ^{1}/$_{16}$ inch (see figs. M2 and M3).

Step 6.
With a ^{1}/$_8$-inch brad-point bit, perpendicular to the side of the body, drill the nostril holes to a depth of ^{1}/$_8$ inch (see figs. M2 and M3).

Step 7.
Mark and carve the mouth in accordance with the Type A method.

Step 8.
On the centerline of the snout, mark the spot for the hole for the nasal horn (see fig. M3).

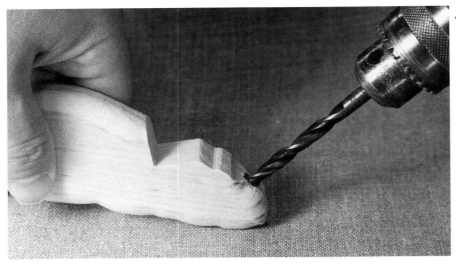

Step 9.
With a ¼-inch brad-point bit at an angle of 90 degrees to the plane of the nose, drill the hole for the horn ¼ inch deep.

Step 10.
Mark the spots on either side of the head for the two side horns (see fig. M3).

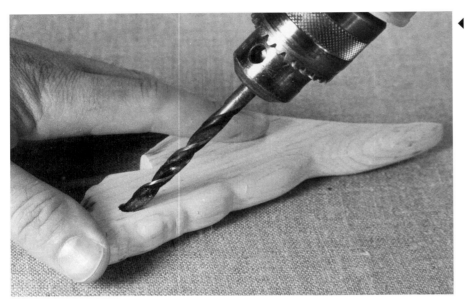

Step 11.
With a ¼-inch brad-point bit, at the angles designated, drill the holes for the side horns to depths of ⅛ inch (see fig. M3).

Step 12.
Being careful not to break the edge at the point where the neck frill will contact the body, sand the body to a fine finish.

Step 13.
Lay out the frill pattern (see fig. M4) on the designated piece of stock with the grain running from top to bottom.

Step 14.
Cut out the basic frill shape with a band saw. When cutting out the inside slot that will fit over the head, be sure to keep the sides parallel and the end squared. The frill should fit snugly over the body, so you might want to cut the opening a little narrower than required and remove the excess by sanding or rasping when fitting it to the body.

◀ Step 15.
Shape the frill to the designated form with a belt sander.

Step 16.
Fine-sand the frill and put it aside.

◀ Step 17.
For the nasal horn, cut a 1¹/₁₆-inch length of ¹/₄-inch-diameter dowel rod.

Step 18.
For the side horns, cut two ¹/₂-inch lengths of ¹/₄-inch-diameter dowel rod.

◀ Step 19.
By sanding, taper one end of each of the three dowel sections to dull points (see fig. M3).

Step 20.
Fine-sand the horns.
Step 21.
Glue the frill to the neck.
Step 22.
With a toothpick, place a small amount of glue in all three holes and affix the horns.
Step 23.
Set aside and let dry.

REAR LEG CONSTRUCTION

The rear legs are made using the Type A construction method (see fig. M5).

Step 1.
Use a $^3/8$-inch brad-point bit to drill the holes through the legs for the axle pegs.

Step 2.
Router the designated areas on each leg with a $^3/8$-inch round-over bit.

Step 3.
Exclusive of the thickness of the heads, cut the axle pegs to a length of $1^1/8$ inches.

FRONT LEG CONSTRUCTION

The front legs are also made using the Type A construction method (see fig. M5).

Step 1.
Use a $^3/16$-inch brad-point bit to drill the holes through the legs for the axle pegs.

Step 2.
Router the designated areas on both legs with a $^1/4$-inch round-over bit.

Step 3.
Exclusive of the thickness of the heads, cut the axle pegs to a length of $^7/8$ inch.

FINISHING AND ASSEMBLY

Step 1.
Finish as desired.

Step 2.
Assemble as per basic Type A leg construction.

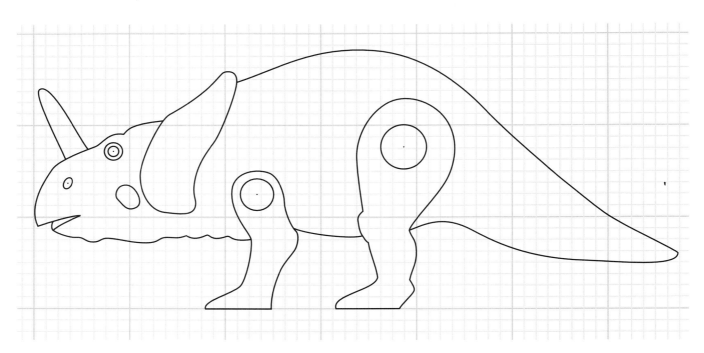

FIGURE M1. PLAN OF COMPLETED MONOCLONIUS (FULL-SCALE)

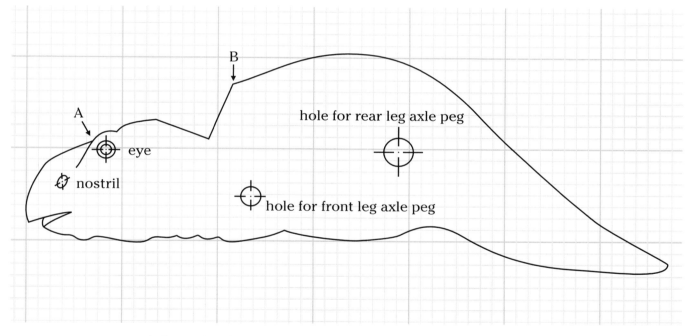

FIGURE M2. BODY PATTERN FOR MONOCLONIUS

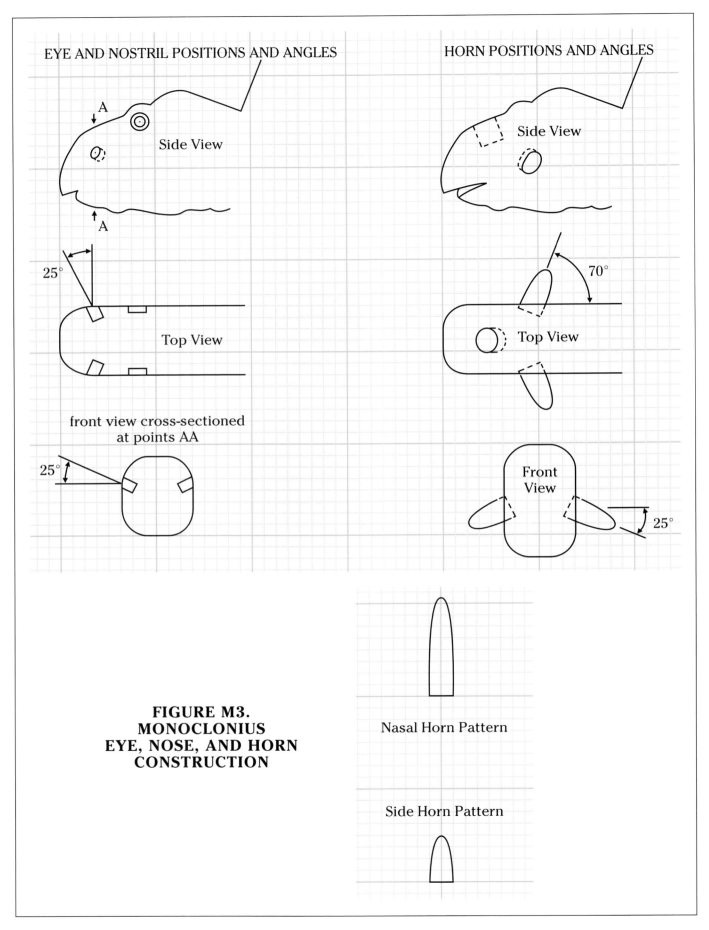

EYE AND NOSTRIL POSITIONS AND ANGLES

Side View

25°

Top View

front view cross-sectioned
at points AA

25°

HORN POSITIONS AND ANGLES

Side View

70°

Top View

Front
View

25°

Nasal Horn Pattern

Side Horn Pattern

**FIGURE M3.
MONOCLONIUS
EYE, NOSE, AND HORN
CONSTRUCTION**

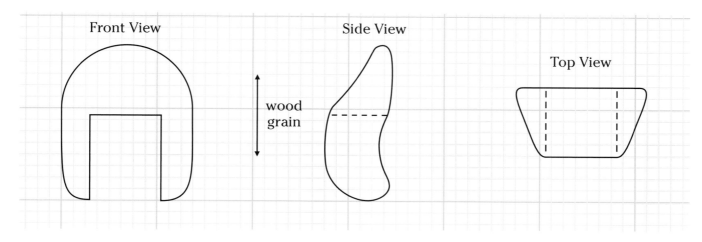

FIGURE M4. MONOCLONIUS FRILL PATTERN

FIGURE M5. MONOCLONIUS LEG PATTERNS

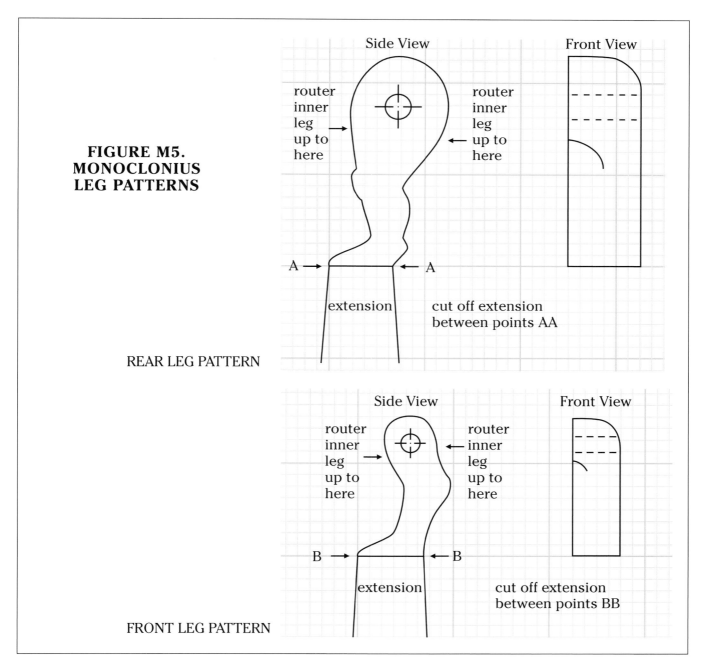

Styracosaurus albertensis

Styracosaurus (sty-RAK-uh-sawr-us): "Spiked lizard"
Order: Ornithischia
Suborder: Ceratopsia
Family: Ceratopsidae
Genus: *Styracosaurus*
Species: *Styracosaurus albertensis*

Close relatives: Monoclonius and Brachyceratops
Length: 18 feet (5.5 meters)
Height: 6 feet (1.8 meters) at the shoulder
Weight: Up to 3 tons (2.7 metric tons)

Styracosaurus, like its close relative Monoclonius, was also a member of the family Ceratopsidae. These animals evolved in Asia and eventually spread to North America to become one of the most successful groups of dinosaurs ever to exist. They were also among the very last to become extinct. Styracosaurus remains come from the Upper Cretaceous Oldman Formation, Red Deer River, Alberta, Canada.

Like Monoclonius, with which it shared the landscape, Styracosaurus was a short-frilled Ceratopsid, and its basic physical characteristics, diet, and lifestyle were the same. The primary feature that distinguished it from other family members was its unique set of horns. Styracosaurus had a long nasal horn measuring about 2 feet in length, and six large horns and a few smaller ones projected from the edge of the frill.

The purpose of Styracosaurus's frill horns has been questioned. One authority sees them as strictly for display to intimidate. Still, on an extremely movable head being tossed from side to side, they could cause considerable damage. Even serving in a passive role, they would certainly deter a predator from trying to bite the neck.

BODY CONSTRUCTION

Step 1.
Follow Steps 1 to 3 as per Camptosaurus (see figs. S1 and S2).
Note: An alternative pattern, Figure S3, is included if you wish to make the Styracosaurus with its tail held higher off the ground.

Step 2.
Using a $^3/_8$-inch round-over bit, router the designated areas on the body. Do not router from the point just in front of the eye bulges back through the spot the frill will fit over (see fig. S2).

Step 3.
With a $^3/_8$-inch brad-point bit, drill both the front and rear leg holes at a 90-degree angle through the body.

Step 4.
With a $^3/_{16}$-inch brad-point bit, perpendicular to the side of the body, drill the eye holes to a depth of $^1/_{16}$ inch (see fig. S4).

Step 5.
With a $^1/_8$-inch brad-point bit, at the center point of the round and

at a 45-degree angle to the side of the body, drill the nostril holes to depths of $^1/_8$ inch (see fig. S4).

Step 6.
Mark and carve the mouth in accordance with the Type A method (see fig. S2).

Step 7.
On the centerline of the nose, mark the spot for the hole for the nasal horn (see fig. S4).

Step 8.
With a $^1/_4$-inch brad-point bit, at the designated angle, drill the hole in the nose $^1/_4$ inch deep.

Step 9.
From a $^1/_4$-inch-diameter dowel rod, cut a $1^1/_8$-inch length for the nasal horn. Note that all horns are made in the same way as those for Monoclonius.

Step 10.
Shape the tip of the horn.

Step 11.
Being careful not to break the edges where the frill will fit over the body, sand the body to a fine finish.

Step 12.
Cut out the basic shape of the neck frill (see fig. S5) with a band saw. Follow the same procedures described in Step 14 of the Monoclonius body construction section.

Step 13.
With a belt sander, shape the frill to the intermediate stage shown in the photograph. Basically, at this point, leave a $^1/_4$-inch-wide flat surface around the edge of the frill.

REQUIRED MATERIALS

Body: One $7^1/_4$ x $3^3/_4$ x $^3/_4$-inch piece of stock
Rear legs: Two 8 x $1^1/_2$ x $^3/_4$-inch pieces of stock
Front legs: Two $7^1/_4$ x $1^1/_8$ x $^3/_4$-inch pieces of stock
Frill: One $1^1/_2$ x $1^1/_2$ x $^3/_4$-inch piece of stock
Horns: $3^1/_2$ inches of $^1/_4$-inch-diameter dowel rod, $4^1/_2$ inches of $^3/_{16}$-inch-diameter dowel rod, and 1 inch of $^1/_8$-inch-diameter dowel rod
Other: Four $^3/_8$-inch-diameter axle pegs for the legs

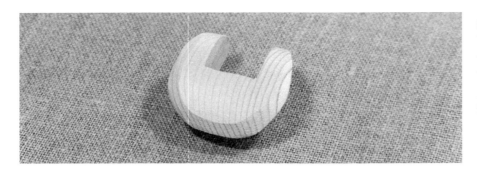

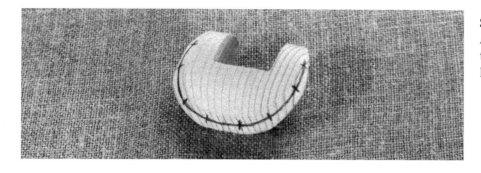

Step 14.
At the designated locations around the frill, mark the spots for the holes for the horns (see fig. S6).

Step 15.
With a ¹/₄-inch brad-point bit, at the required angle, drill the two top center holes in the frill to a depth of ¹/₄ inch each.

Step 16.
With a ³/₁₆-inch brad-point bit, at the required angles, drill the next four holes in the frill (two on either side of those just completed) to a depth of ¹/₄ inch.

Step 17.
With a ¹/₈-inch brad-point bit, at the designated angle, drill the last two (bottom) holes ¹/₈ inch deep.

Step 18.
From the ¹/₄-inch-diameter dowel rod, cut two pieces 1¹/₈ inches long.

Step 19.
From the ³/₁₆-inch-diameter dowel rod, cut four pieces 1 inch long.

Step 20.
From the ¹/₈-inch-diameter dowel rod, cut two pieces ³/₈ inch long.

Step 21.
Taper one end of each of the eight dowel sections just cut to a rounded point.

Step 22.
Without gluing, fit the horns to the frill to check the angles. Adjust as necessary.

Step 23.
Finish shaping the frill with the belt sander by rounding and tapering the edge the holes are in.

Step 24.
Fine-sand the frill.

Step 25.
Once you are sure of the fit, glue the frill to the body.

Step 26.
Place a small amount of glue in each hole in the frill, insert the dowel horns in their proper place, align them, and let dry.

Step 27.
Place a small amount of glue in the hole for the nasal horn and insert the dowel horn into it. Align the horn and let the glue dry.

FRONT AND REAR LEG CONSTRUCTION
Both the front and rear legs (see fig. S7) are made using the Type A construction method.
Step 1.
Use a $^3/_8$-inch brad-point bit to drill the holes through the legs for the axle pegs.
Step 2.
Router the designated areas on all four legs with a $^3/_8$-inch round-over bit.

Step 3.
Exclusive of the thickness of the heads, cut all four axle pegs to lengths of $1^1/_8$ inches.

FINISHING AND ASSEMBLY
Step 1.
Finish as desired.

Step 2.
Assemble as per basic Type A leg construction.

FIGURE S1. PLAN OF COMPLETED STYRACOSAURUS (FULL-SCALE)

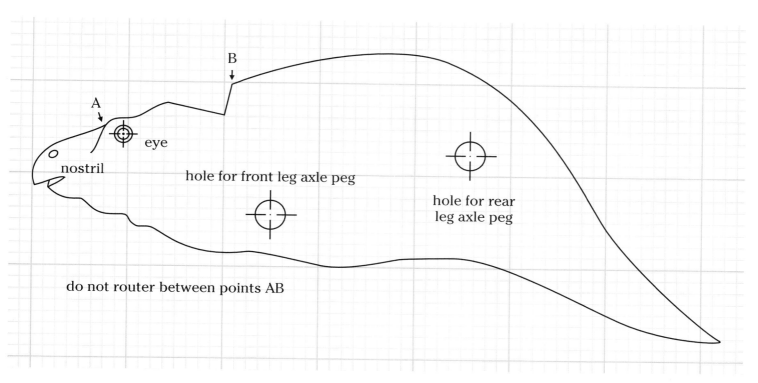

FIGURE S2. BODY PATTERN FOR STYRACOSAURUS

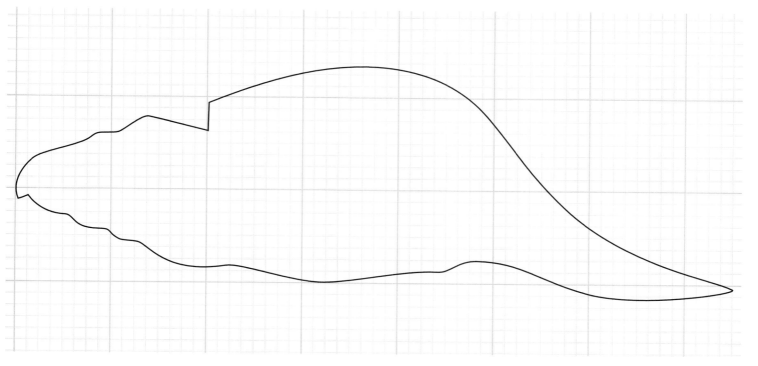

FIGURE S3. ALTERNATE BODY PATTERN FOR STYRACOSAURUS

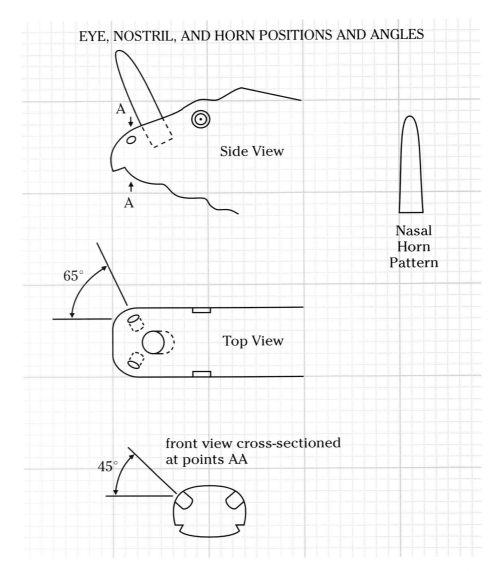

EYE, NOSTRIL, AND HORN POSITIONS AND ANGLES

Side View

Nasal Horn Pattern

65°

Top View

front view cross-sectioned at points AA

45°

FIGURE S4. STYRACOSAURUS EYE, NOSE, AND HORN CONSTRUCTION

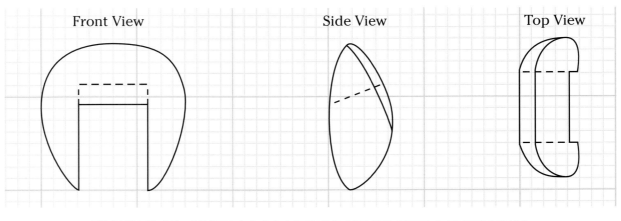

Front View

Side View

Top View

FIGURE S5. STYRACOSAURUS NECK FRILL PATTERN

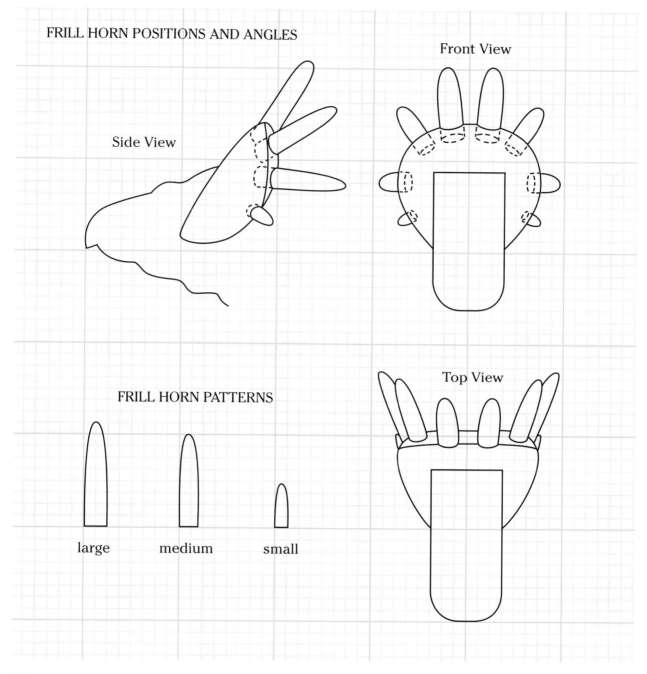

FRILL HORN POSITIONS AND ANGLES

Front View

Side View

FRILL HORN PATTERNS

large   medium   small

Top View

FIGURE S6. STYRACOSAURUS FRILL HORN PATTERNS AND CONSTRUCTION

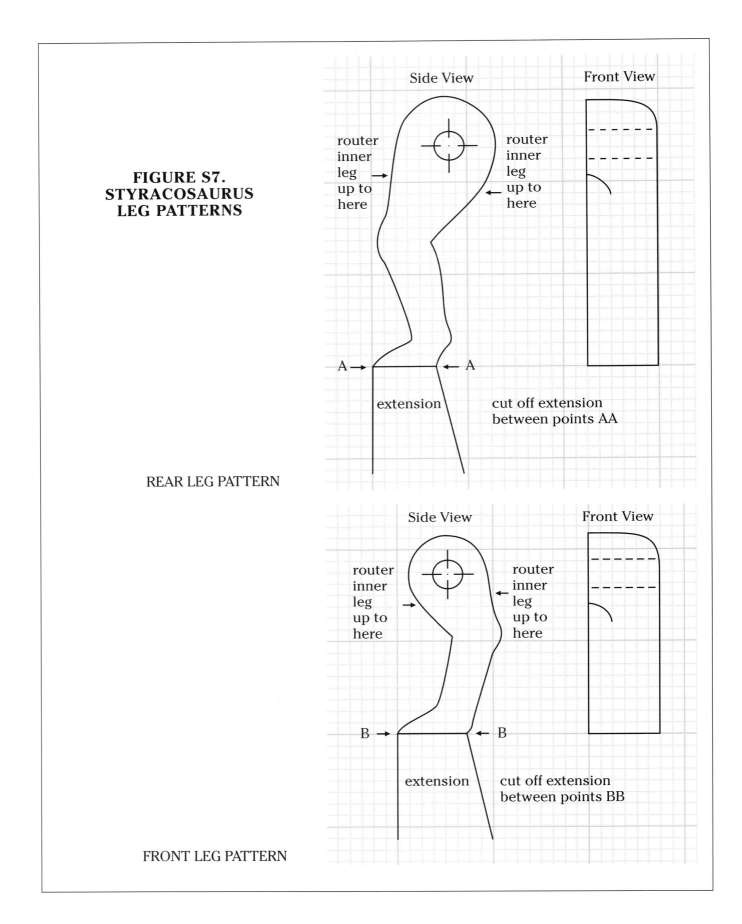

**FIGURE S7.
STYRACOSAURUS
LEG PATTERNS**

Side View

Front View

router inner leg up to here

router inner leg up to here

A →   ← A

extension

cut off extension between points AA

REAR LEG PATTERN

Side View

Front View

router inner leg up to here

router inner leg up to here

B →   ← B

extension

cut off extension between points BB

FRONT LEG PATTERN

Apatosaurus ajax (Brontosaurus)

Apatosaurus (ah-PAT-uh-sawr-us): "Deceptive lizard"
Brontosaurus (bron-tuh-SAWR-us): "Thunder lizard"
Order: Saurischia
Suborder: Sauropodomorpha
Infraorder: Sauropoda
Family: Diplodocidae or Atlantosauridae
Genus: *Apatosaurus*
Species: *Apatosaurus ajax*

Close relatives: Diplodocus, Barosaurus, and Mamenchisaurus
Length: 70 to 80 feet (21 to 25 meters)
Height: 15 feet (4.5 meters) at the shoulder
Weight: 20 to 40 tons (18 to 36 metric tons)

This best known of all dinosaurs has suffered severe identity problems. First discovered in 1877, it was named Apatosaurus. Another set of remains, unearthed in 1879, was thought to represent a different animal and labeled Brontosaurus. Eventually it became apparent the two fossil skeletons were, in fact, from the same type of creature. As a result, the first applied name is considered the correct one, rather than that which is better known. To further confuse the issue, some authorities maintain that both Atlantosaurus and Titanosaurus are also the same as Apatosaurus.

Another problem with Apatosaurus, only recently rectified, concerns its proper head. Traditionally, this dinosaur was displayed with the skull of a Camarosaurid (a very different Sauropod), which was not actually found with the rest of the Apatosaur skeleton. In fact, only one real Apatosaurus skull has ever been discovered. It is similar to that of Diplodocus.

The first Apatosaurus remains came from the Late Jurassic Morrison Formation of Colorado. Apatosaurus has since been found in Montana, Wyoming, Utah, Oklahoma, and Baja California, as well as Europe.

In terms of both length and weight, Apatosaurus was one of the largest dinosaurs. Primarily quadrupedal, it had a massive body with a 30-foot tail and a 20-foot neck supported by four huge, pillarlike legs. The front legs, however, were much shorter than the rear. Each foot had five toes and measured 3 feet across. On the innermost toe of each front foot, there was a long, spikelike claw, and the first three toes in back had claws of relatively moderate length. The remaining toes were clawless.

The head of this animal was incredibly small in relationship with the rest of its body. The snout was elongated, with the nostrils set far back and high on the skull. The mouth contained peglike teeth located only in front. About the size of a human fist, Apatosaurus's brain was merely $1/100,000$ of its total body weight. Still, while its mental capacity may not have matched its size, it is believed this dinosaur did have very keen senses of sight, smell, and hearing. Apatosaurus's skin was thick and leathery.

As with the other dinosaurs, controversy rages over whether Apatosaurus was cold- or warm-blooded. Because of its great size and numerous unusual features, both schools of thought look to this creature as an example to support their beliefs. Traditionally, Apatosaurus has been thought of as cold-blooded and reptilian. It is argued that, because of its small head and small number of highly specialized teeth, the beast could not possibly have eaten enough to maintain a high metabolism.

Proponents of warm-bloodedness counter with several assertions supporting their opinions. To begin with, they state that if Apatosaurus's body temperature dropped only a degree or two (a normal occurrence with all reptiles in the cool of the evening), given their mass, it would take an incredible amount of time to recharge in sunlight and reestablish the required level of body heat. These scientists believe that if cold-blooded, these gigantic animals could not have mustered enough energy even to stand, let alone move about.

These same authorities also believe that despite the small head and odd teeth, Apatosaurus could eat enough to fuel a high metabolism. Granted, it is estimated that they needed 500 to 1,000 pounds of plant food daily, and they would have had to spend their entire waking hours eating, but it is possible that they could have gotten the necessary nutrients. In essence, these creatures had gizzards in which gastroliths (swallowed grinding stones) in conjunction with chemical enzymes seriously aided digestion. At the same time, the construction of the nasal passages would have allowed the beast to keep breathing without interrupting its dinner. Basically, Apatosaurus could constantly eat and breathe at the same time.

The cold-blooded supporters counter that while ectothermic, Apatosaurus was really homeothermic. This means their great size would have worked in favor of their being cold-blooded instead of against it. Essentially, their body mass was so great, it never had time to cool, or if it did, it was so minimal it did not matter.

The other great debate over these docile plant-eaters concerns the nature of their environment. Traditionally, Apatosaurus is viewed as having wallowed around in swamps and lakes munching on soft water vegetation. It followed a semiaquatic lifestyle. Because of its weight in association with a supposedly insufficient skeletal structure, many assert this creature could not even support itself on land but needed water to buoy it up. The long neck was employed as a snorkel to raise the head up from deep water to breathe. To these authorities, the high position of the nostrils clearly indicates this practice. The lack of molars means they could eat only soft aquatic plants. Also, Apatosaurus is considered to have been basically defenseless. As a result, these authorities believe, it used the water as a barrier to protect itself from carnivores.

Newer theories are completely polarized from those just outlined, and supporting arguments are plentiful. To begin with, it is pointed out that the skeleton was more than capable of supporting the body mass. The legs were similar to those of an elephant, and the spinal column was perforated with load-lightening holes, which greatly reduced its weight. In fact, the weight of the frame was so diminished that it argues against an aquatic lifestyle. The animal would have been so buoyant, it would have floated uncontrollably. It was simply too light.

Another argument against life in a watery habitat centers on Apatosaurus's inability to breathe in it. In essence, if the head on the long neck were used as a snorkel with the body 20 feet below the surface, the water pressure would be too great to allow the lungs to expand and fill.

Those who argue against aquatic dwelling opt for an upland or forest habitat instead. There, these gentle giants are thought to have been the giraffes of the dinosaur world. Using their long necks, they browsed for food among the highest treetops. Their peglike teeth raked coarse pine needles, leaves, and twigs off branches and into their gizzards for digestion. It is even maintained by many that these huge beasts could extend their height by rearing up on their hind legs to reach food farther up.

Socially, Apatosaurs lived in herds. This is supported by fossilized footprints showing many individuals moving in the same direction at the same time. Traveling in herds may be a reason the tails were held off the ground. It prevented their being stepped on. The ancient tracks also show that the young ambled along in the middle of the group, undoubtedly for protection.

Although many scientists feel these creatures were incapable of self-defense, new opinion suggests that Apatosaurus was more than capable of taking care of itself. Its immense size alone was enough to deter many would-be attackers. Herding offered safety in numbers, and only the most hungry and enterprising packs of Allosaurs or Ceratosaurs would consider assaulting such a formation. Even on a one-to-one basis, the giant Sauropod could hold its own.

Its tough, leathery skin helped protect it, and the long, powerful tail offered an effective whiplike weapon. Furthermore, a number of authorities theorize that the ability to rear up also aided in a fight. Pushing up onto its hind legs, Apatosaurus could then drop down onto its front ones and crush an attacker with its great weight.

A final controversy surrounds Apatosaurus young. While most scientists think they hatched from eggs, a few authorities believe that live birth was the means of delivery. Supporting the egg theory are the nearly round, sandpaper-finished, 10-inch (25-centimeter) specimens found in France and thought to be from the Sauropod Hypselosaurus. If hatched from eggs, Apatosaurus young were about the size of a modern house cat. This is about the limit, in terms of size, that an egg can accommodate. In turn, this very fact is used by supporters of live birth to advance their claims. They say the eggs and hatchlings were too small for such large animals. The young would not have been able to survive without being stepped on in the herd.

BODY CONSTRUCTION
Step 1.
On the large piece of stock, lay out two body patterns (see fig. AP3) plus the head, neck, and tail patterns (see fig. AP2) with the wood grain running lengthwise for all. On the neck, tail, and one body piece, use an awl to mark the center points for the holes for the leg axle pegs, the joint pivot pins, and the eye on one side.
Step 2.
Using a band saw, cut out the two body sections, the neck, and the tail.

REQUIRED MATERIALS

Body, neck, and tail: One 29 x 5 x $^3/_4$-inch piece of stock
Rear legs: Two 10$^1/_2$ x 2$^3/_4$ x $^3/_4$-inch pieces of stock
Front legs: Two 8 x 1$^1/_8$ x $^3/_4$-inch pieces of stock
Other: Four $^3/_8$-inch-diameter axle pegs for the legs, one 4-inch length of $^5/_{16}$-inch-diameter dowel rod for the tail and neck pins, and one 1$^1/_2$-inch length of $^3/_{16}$-inch-diameter dowel rod for the claws

---

Step 3.
After cutting, reverse the pattern for the neck piece to the opposite side and mark the hole for the other eye.

Step 4.
Determine which side of each body piece will be the outer one when the two sections are put together.

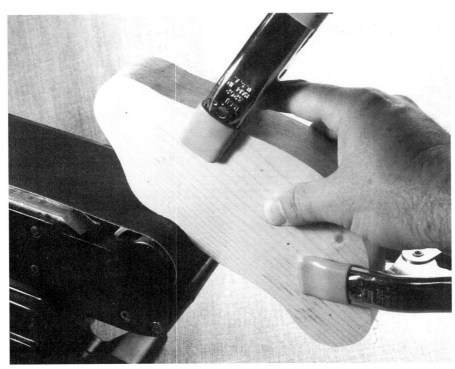

Step 5.

Without gluing, clamp the two body pieces together, and with a belt or drum sander, sand so the edges of the two pieces are flush with each other.

Step 6.

With a ³⁄₈-inch round-over bit, router completely around the edge of the side of each body part that will face out when assembled.

Step 7.

With the same bit, router the designated areas on the neck and tail pieces (see fig. AP2).

At this point, there are several different methods you can use to create the sockets in the body for the neck and tail pieces, depending on your ability and whether you have a Forstner drill bit.

Method A
Step 8A.

Place the neck and tail sections in their proper positions over the unrouted side of each body half, and outline the round joint ends. When the two body halves are placed together, the circles on each should align.

Step 9A.

With a ³/₄-inch straight or rabbeting router bit, remove the wood from within the circles just drawn on the body pieces. The maximum depth of cut is ³/₈ inch for all circles. Router all four areas at the same time so that the cut depths are exactly the same. The cuts need not follow the lines of the circles exactly, but they should be as close as possible. Any remaining wood can be removed by hand with a chisel. Proceed with Step 10.

Method B
Step 8B.

Align the two body halves and, without gluing, clamp them together. With a ¹/₁₆-inch bit, at the points designated for the neck and tail pivot pins, drill a hole completely through the body.

Step 9B.

Unclamp the two halves. On the inside of each body half, using the small hole as a guide, drill all four socket areas (see figs. AP3 and AP4) to a depth of ³/₈ inch with a 2-inch Forstner bit making a flat-bottomed hole and a drill press. Proceed with Step 10.

Method C
◀ **Step 8C.**

This method uses a 1-inch Forstner drill bit and drill press. You do not need to drill the ¹/₁₆-inch center guide hole for this process. Set the drill press to bore a hole ³/₈ inch deep.

Step 9C.

Following the lines marked for the sockets, make a series of overlapping holes until all unwanted wood is removed from the socket areas. Proceed with Step 10.

Step 10.

Align the two body halves, glue them together, and clamp under moderate pressure.

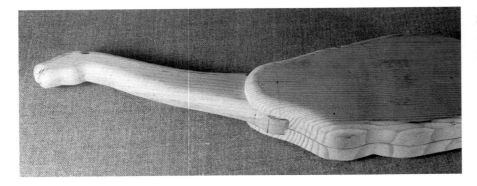

Step 11.
Fit the neck piece into the appropriate socket and properly align it.

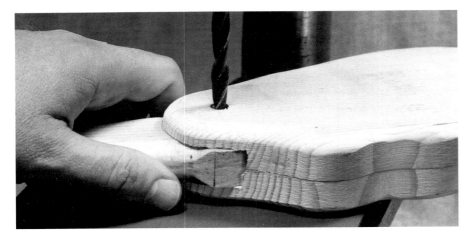

Step 12.
With a ⁵/₁₆-inch brad-point bit, drill the hole for the dowel pin completely through the body and neck piece at the same time.

Step 13.
Repeat Steps 11 and 12 for the tail section.

Step 14.
With a ³/₈-inch brad-point bit, drill the front and rear leg holes at a 90-degree angle through the body.

Step 15.
With a ³/₁₆-inch brad-point bit, at a 90-degree angle to the side of the neck piece, drill the eye holes to a depth of ¹/₈ inch (see figs. AP2 and AP6).

Step 16.
Locate and mark the points for the nostril holes on the top of the head (see figs. AP2 and AP6).

Step 17.
With a ¹/₈-inch brad-point bit, at the angles indicated (see fig. AP6), drill the two nostril holes to depths of ¹/₈ inch. At this point you will carve the mouth, then return to body construction.

CARVING THE MOUTH
This open, Type C mouth (see fig. AP7) is used only for this particular pattern. A series of only two cuts is required, which will create a V notch from the front of the mouth. Much of this effect will have already been created by the cutting out of the head and neck with the band saw.

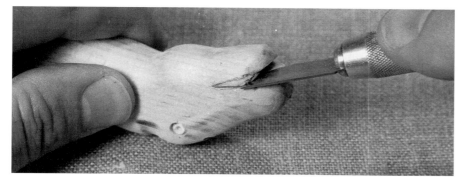

Step 1.
From the very front, make a cut at an angle following the line of the upper mouth as it continues back.

◀ **Step 2.**
Repeat the process along the lower mouth line.

Step 3.
Carve out the wood between the two cuts.

Step 4.
Keep repeating this process until a V is formed with its apex about half-way along the length of the mouth.

Step 5.
Upon reaching the halfway point, finish carving to each corner as if this were a Type A mouth.

Step 6.
Even out any irregularities with the knife or rifflers.

Step 7.
Sand the areas from which wood was removed.

Completed Type C Mouth

FINISHING AND ASSEMBLING THE BODY

Step 1.
Sand the neck and tail pieces to a fine finish.

Step 2.
Finish the neck and tail pieces as desired. *Do not* finish the body at this point.

Step 3.
Cut two small squares of inner tube roughly ½ x ¾ inch, and place one in the back of each socket in the body.

Step 4.
Cut two lengths of ⁵⁄₁₆-inch-diameter dowel that are slightly longer than the width of the body.

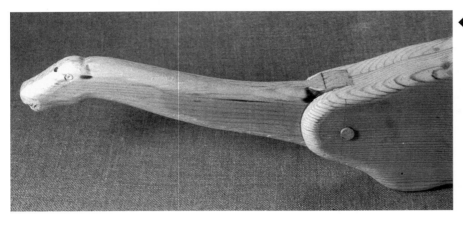

◀ Step 5.
Without gluing, fit the neck and tail sections in place and attempt to fit the ⁵⁄₁₆-inch-diameter dowel pegs in place. There should be a snug fit with the inner tube, creating friction on the neck and tail that will keep them in position when posed. If the fit is too tight, remove a small amount of wood from the back of the socket. If it is too loose, double the thickness of the inner tube. When the desired tension is attained, glue the inner tube pieces in place with contact cement.

Step 6.
Fine-sand the body.

Step 7.
Be careful not to get any glue on the neck and tail pieces, or they will not be movable. Insert the pegs through the body and neck and the body and tail, and glue in place.

◀ Step 8.
Sand the extended ends of the pegs flush with the body.

Step 9.
If the dowel pegs are of a different wood than the body and a natural finish is desired, stain the ends of the pegs to match.

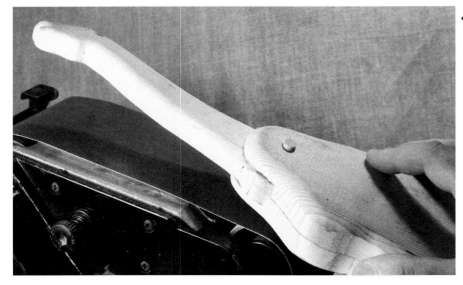

LEG CONSTRUCTION

Both the front and rear legs (see figs. AP8 and AP9) are made using the Type A construction method. There are, however, some additional procedures required for the front legs.

• Use a ³/₈-inch brad-point bit to drill the holes through the legs for the axle pegs.

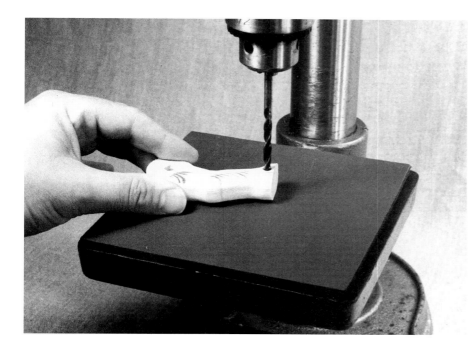

• Use a ³/₈-inch round-over bit to router the designated areas on the legs.

Step 1.
Mark the point on the inside of each front foot for the claw.

◀ **Step 2.**
With a ³/₁₆-inch brad-point bit, at a 90-degree angle, drill the hole for the claw in each foot to a depth of ¹/₄ inch.

Step 3.
From ³/₁₆-inch-diameter dowel rod, cut two pieces ¹/₂ inch long.

Step 4.
By sanding, round one end of each dowel piece.

Step 5.
Glue the dowel claws in place.

Step 6.
Exclusive of the thickness of the heads, cut all four axle pegs to lengths of 1¹/₂ inches.

Step 7.
Proceed as per basic Type A instructions.

FINISHING AND ASSEMBLY

Step 1.
Being careful not to get stain, varnish, or other finish on the areas already done or in the neck and tail joints, finish the body section as desired.

Step 2.
Assemble as per basic Type A leg construction.

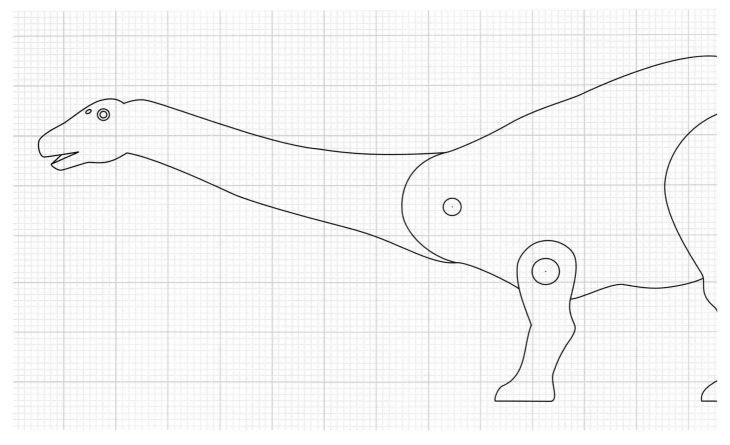

**FIGURE AP1. PLAN OF COMPLETED APATOSAURUS
(60% SCALE)**

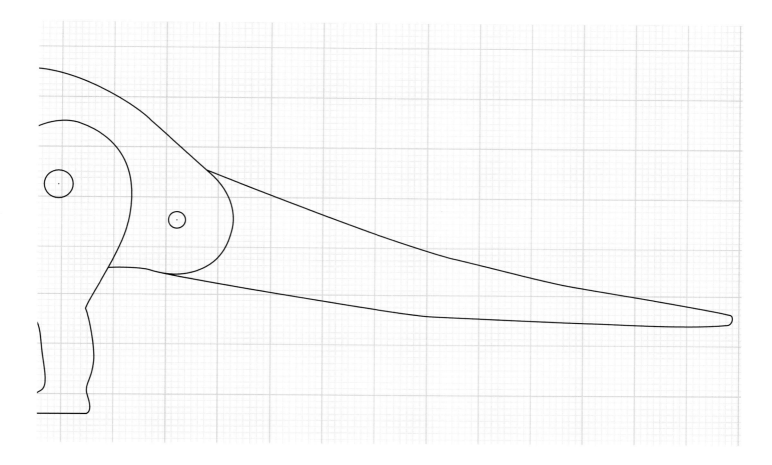

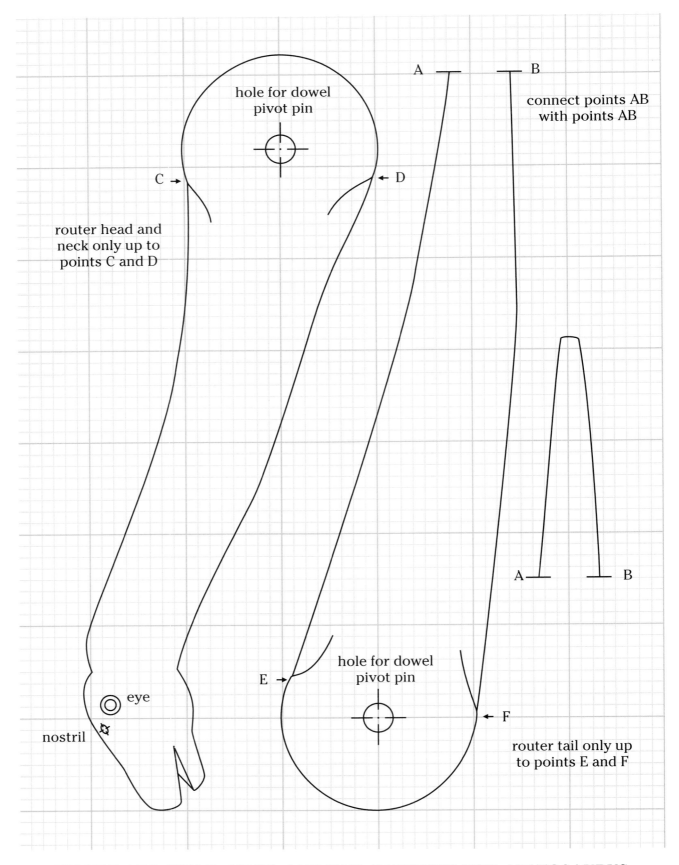

FIGURE AP2. HEAD, NECK, AND TAIL PATTERNS FOR APATOSAURUS

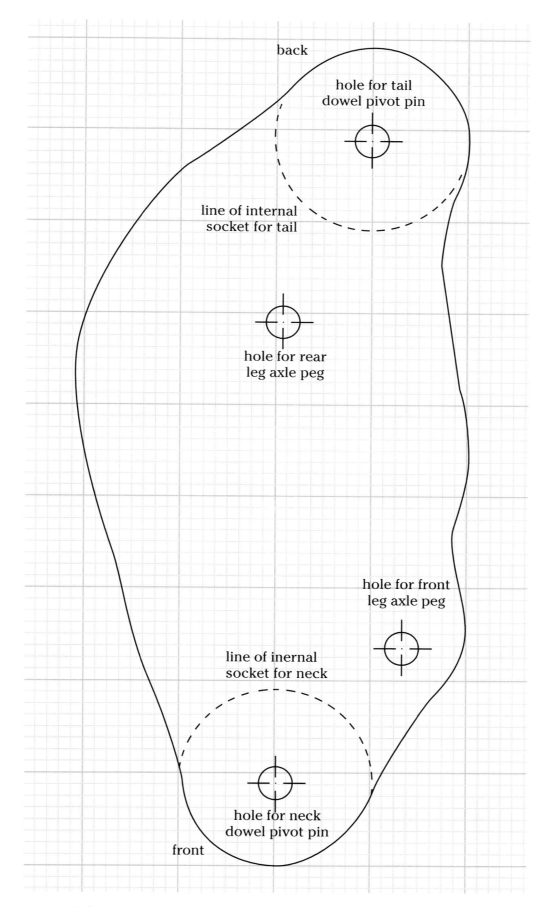

FIGURE AP3. BODY PATTERN FOR APATOSAURUS

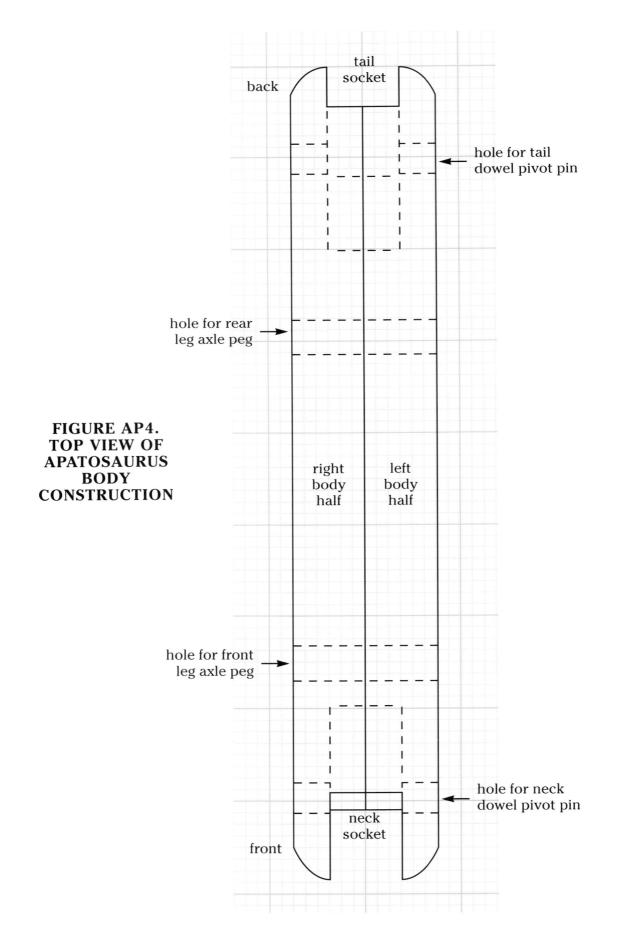

back

tail
socket

hole for tail
dowel pivot pin

hole for rear
leg axle peg

**FIGURE AP4.
TOP VIEW OF
APATOSAURUS
BODY
CONSTRUCTION**

right
body
half

left
body
half

hole for front
leg axle peg

hole for neck
dowel pivot pin

neck
socket

front

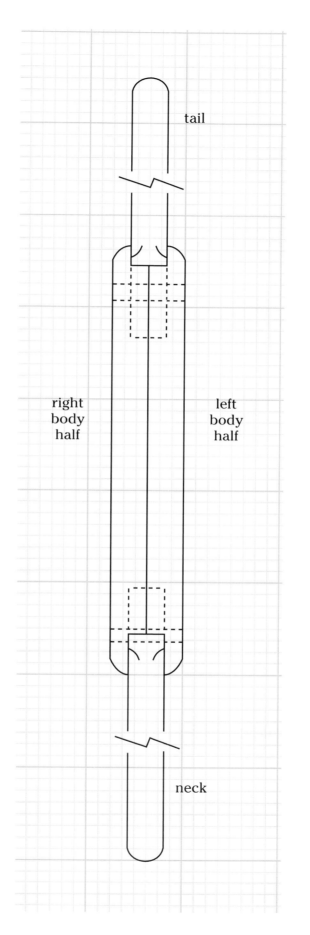

tail

right
body
half

left
body
half

neck

**FIGURE AP5.
TOP VIEW OF
APATOSAURUS
NECK, TAIL,
AND BODY
ASSEMBLY
(NOT FULL-SCALE)**

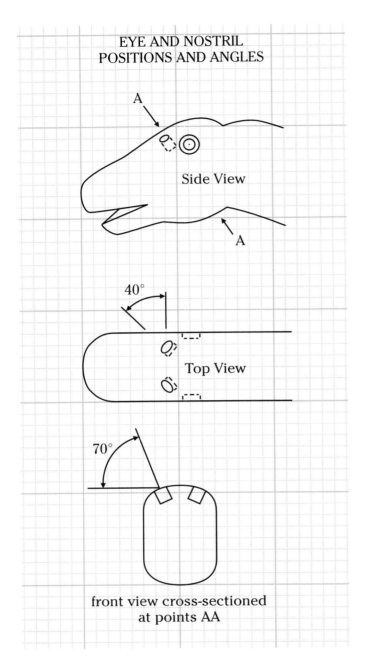

EYE AND NOSTRIL
POSITIONS AND ANGLES

A

Side View

40°

Top View

70°

front view cross-sectioned
at points AA

**FIGURE AP6.
APATOSAURUS
EYE AND NOSTRIL CONSTRUCTION**

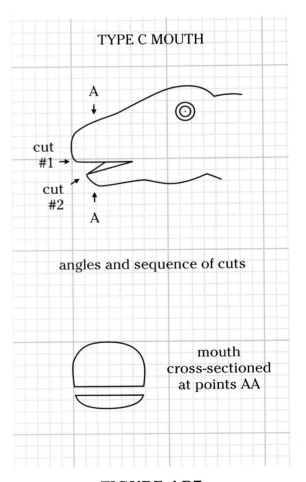

TYPE C MOUTH

A

cut
#1

cut
#2

A

angles and sequence of cuts

mouth
cross-sectioned
at points AA

**FIGURE AP7.
CARVING
APATOSAURUS MOUTH**

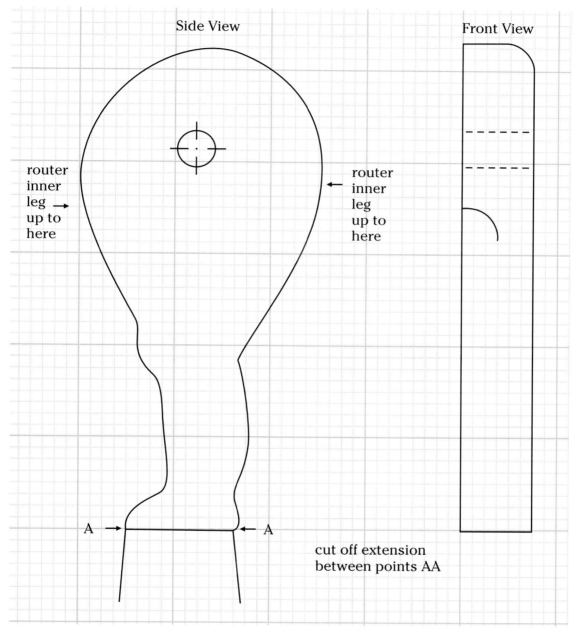

Side View

Front View

router
inner
leg →
up to
here

← router
inner
leg
up to
here

A →

← A

cut off extension
between points AA

FIGURE AP8. APATOSAURUS REAR LEG PATTERN

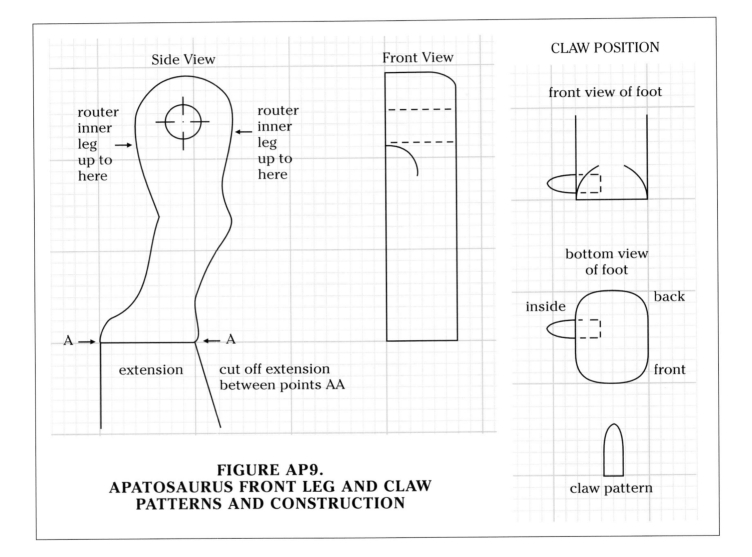

Side View

router
inner
leg
up to
here

router
inner
leg
up to
here

A →

← A

extension

cut off extension
between points AA

Front View

CLAW POSITION

front view of foot

bottom view
of foot

inside

back

front

claw pattern

**FIGURE AP9.
APATOSAURUS FRONT LEG AND CLAW
PATTERNS AND CONSTRUCTION**

Plateosaurus quenstedti

Plateosaurus (PLAY-tee-uh-sawr-us): "Flat lizard"
Order: Saurischia
Suborder: Sauropodomorpha
Infraorder: Prosauropoda
Family: Plateosauridae
Genus: *Plateosaurus*
Species: *Plateosaurus quenstedti*

Close relatives: Anchisaurus and Riojasaurus
Length: Up to 26 feet (8 meters)
Height: Up to 16.4 feet (5 meters) when on rear legs

Plateosaurus remains were first discovered in the Keuper Sandstone Formations of Trossingen, Germany. Since, additional fossils have been found in France, England, Switzerland, South Africa, and Nova Scotia, Canada. This Upper Triassic creature was long considered a direct ancestor of the later Sauropods such as Diplodocus and Apatosaurus. It is now believed to be only a distant uncle and part of a separate lineage that died out.

Like Sauropods, Plateosaurus had a rather bulky torso, long tail, and a small head at the end of a fairly long neck. The body was carried around on two long, massive, powerful hind legs and two shorter, but also strong, front ones. All four of the very broad feet possessed five long toes. In front, on the "thumb," there was a long, curved claw. In addition, the second and third "fingers" displayed long, straight claws. The clawless fourth and fifth digits were much reduced in size. On the rear feet, all the toes had long claws except the smallest.

The jaws of the small head held flat, serrated, triangular teeth, thus the animal's name. Although their pointed shape indicates this animal evolved from a meat-eating ancestor, and occasionally may have

supplemented its diet with a small animal, Plateosaurus was primarily a planteater. The bulky body suggests the development of a digestive tract capable of handling very tough, fibrous vegetation, so chewing with these teeth that were ill suited for plant matter was unnecessary. In essence, internally, there were large fermentation chambers that acted in association with gizzard stones to break down foods.

The difference in length between the front and rear legs in conjunction with the long, heavy tail that could function as a counterbalance indicates that Plateosaurus could easily rise up on its hind legs to a bipedal stance. Some authorities believe this was done only occasionally and only for the purpose of reaching higher-growing plants. Actual movement was conducted on all fours. Other scientists believe that Plateosaurus was equally at home walking on two or four legs, and that to escape predators, the beast could run very fast on only its rear legs.

There is scholarly discussion, as well, over the function of the long thumb claws on the front feet. Some see them as tools used for rooting for food or hooking branches to pull them to the mouth. It is also said they could have been effective defensive weapons for jabbing attacking predators. One noted authority maintains Plateosaurus could rear up and, in this position, slash with its front feet and kick with its rear ones.

Still, these were generally peaceful creatures that probably dwelt in herds. Moving along in search of food, they could eat both low- and high-growing vegetation as they kept a watchful eye out for roving predators.

REQUIRED MATERIALS

Body, neck, and tail: One 20 x $1^1/_2$ x $^1/_2$-inch or one $8^1/_2$ x 3 x $^1/_2$-inch piece of stock

Rear legs: Two $7^1/_2$ x 1 x $^1/_2$-inch pieces of stock

Front legs: Two 7 x $^3/_4$ x $^3/_8$-inch pieces of stock

Other: Two $^3/_8$-inch-diameter axle pegs for the rear legs, one $1^1/_2$-inch length of $^1/_8$-inch-diameter dowel rod for the front legs, and 3 inches of $^1/_3$-inch-diameter dowel rod for the neck and tail joint pins

---

BODY CONSTRUCTION

Plateosaurus body construction is identical to that for Apatosaurus, but because the model is smaller, different size bits are required. Read the following instructions outlining procedure variations in conjunction with those for the Apatosaurus.

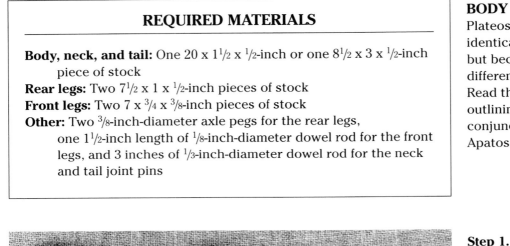

Plateosaurus tail cutout with extension

Step 1.
Follow Steps 1 to 5 as per Apatosaurus, but leave a 4-inch extension off the neck and tail socket areas to use as a handle when routering.

Step 2.
With a $^1/_4$-inch round-over bit, completely router the edge of what will be the outer surface of each body half.

Step 3.
With the same router bit, router the designated areas on the neck and tail pieces (see fig. PL2). Do not router the area over the eyes or the edges around the circular ends that will fit into the sockets.

Step 4.
Use a band saw to cut off the extensions on the neck and tail pieces.

Step 5.
Align the neck and tail sections in their proper positions over the unroutered side of each body half, and outline the round joint ends. When the two body halves are placed together, the circles on each should align.

Step 6.
At this point, as with Apatosaurus, you can proceed using one of a few methods to create the sockets in the body for the neck and tail

pieces, depending on your ability and the tools on hand.

6A.

If you will be using Method A, routering out the four circular areas to create the sockets in the body for the neck and tail pieces, use a $3/4$-inch straight or rabbeting bit, and cut to a depth of $1/4$ inch.

6B.

If you choose to drill out the sockets, follow Method B, using a 1-inch Forstner bit designed to cut a flat-bottomed hole, and drill to a depth of $1/4$ inch.

Step 7.

Align the two body halves, glue them together, and clamp under moderate pressure.

Step 8.

Fit the neck piece onto the appropriate socket and align properly.

Step 9.

With a $1/4$-inch brad-point bit, drill the hole for the dowel pin completely through the body and neck piece at the same time.

Step 10.

Repeat Steps 8 and 9 for the tail piece.

Step 11.

With a $3/8$-inch brad-point bit (or a bit equivalent to the exact diameter of the axle pegs used), at a 90-degree angle to the side, drill the rear leg hole through the body.

Step 12.

With a $1/8$-inch brad-point bit, perpendicular with the side, drill the front leg hole through the body.

Step 13.

With a $1/8$-inch brad-point bit, at a 90-degree angle to the side of the head, drill the eye holes to a depth of $1/16$ inch (see fig. PL4).

Step 14.

With a $1/16$-inch bit, at the designated angles, drill the nostril holes to a depth of $1/16$ inch (see fig. PL4).

Step 15.

Mark and carve the mouth in accordance with the Type B method (see figs. PL2 and PL4).

Step 16.

Proceed as per instructions under Finishing and Assembling the Body for Apatosaurus, cutting the two inner tube friction pads to $3/8$ x $1/2$ inch. Cut the pivot pins for the neck and tail from $1/4$-inch-diameter dowel rod.

REAR LEG CONSTRUCTION

The rear legs are made using the Type A construction method (see fig. PL5).

Step 1.

Use a $3/8$-inch brad-point bit to drill the holes through the legs for the axle pegs.

Step 2.

Router the designated areas with a $1/4$-inch round-over bit.

Step 3.

Exclusive of the thickness of the head, cut the axle pegs to a length of 1 inch.

FRONT LEG CONSTRUCTION

The front legs are made using the Type B construction method (see fig. PL5).

Step 1.

To accommodate the dowel rod, use a $1/8$-inch brad-point bit to drill a hole $3/16$ inch deep on the inside of each leg.

Step 2.

With a $1/4$-inch round-over bit, router the designated areas on the front legs.

Step 3.

Cut a $1 3/8$-inch length of $1/8$-inch-diameter dowel rod.

FINISHING AND ASSEMBLY

Step 1.

Being careful not to get any stain, varnish, or other finish on the areas already done or in the sockets, finish the body section as desired.

Step 2.

Assemble as per basic Type A and B leg construction.

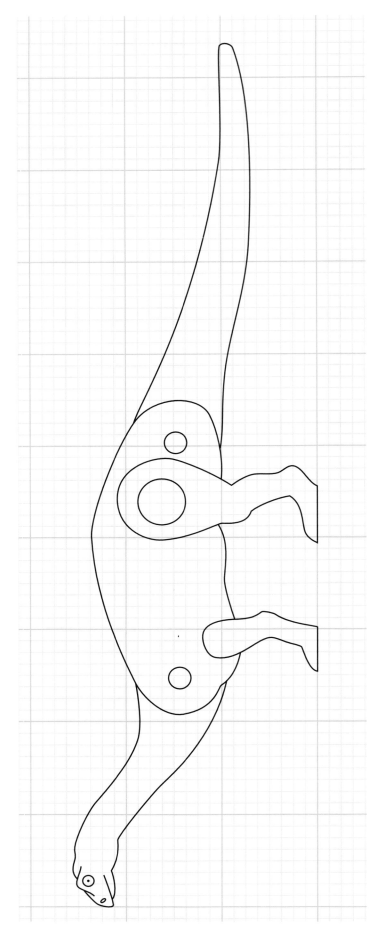

FIGURE PL1. PLAN OF COMPLETED PLATEOSAURUS (FULL-SCALE)

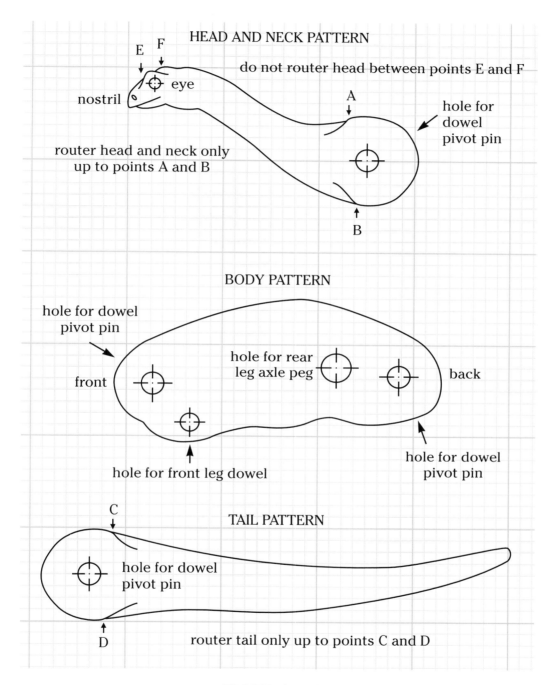

FIGURE PL2.
HEAD, NECK, BODY, AND TAIL PATTERNS FOR PLATEOSAURUS

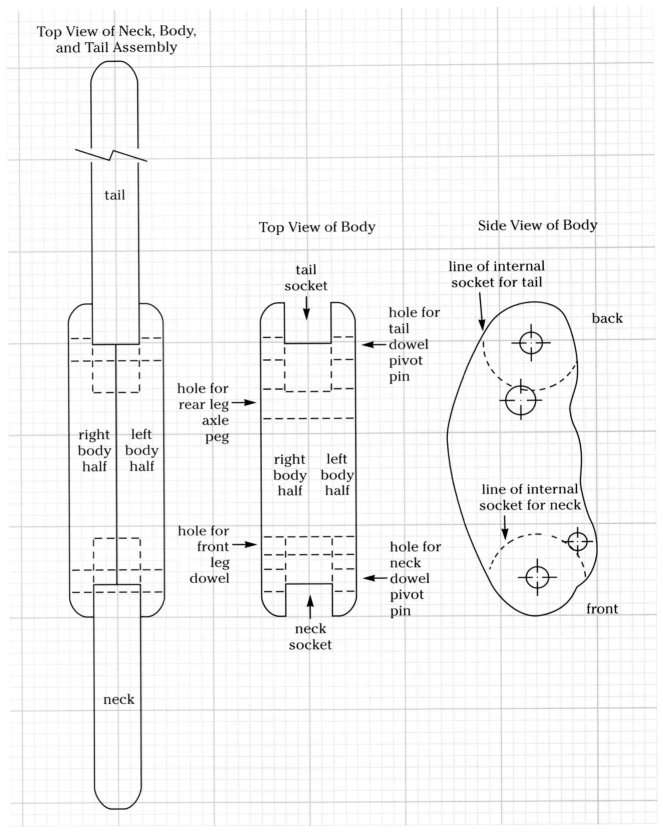

Top View of Neck, Body, and Tail Assembly

tail

right body half

left body half

neck

Top View of Body

tail socket

hole for tail dowel pivot pin

hole for rear leg axle peg

right body half

left body half

hole for front leg dowel

hole for neck dowel pivot pin

neck socket

Side View of Body

line of internal socket for tail

back

line of internal socket for neck

front

FIGURE PL3.
VIEWS OF PLATEOSAURUS BODY AND NECK, TAIL, AND BODY ASSEMBLY

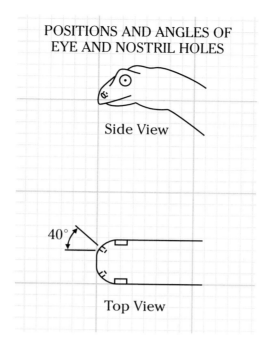

POSITIONS AND ANGLES OF
EYE AND NOSTRIL HOLES

Side View

40°

Top View

**FIGURE PL4.
PLATEOSAURUS
EYE AND NOSE CONSTRUCTION**

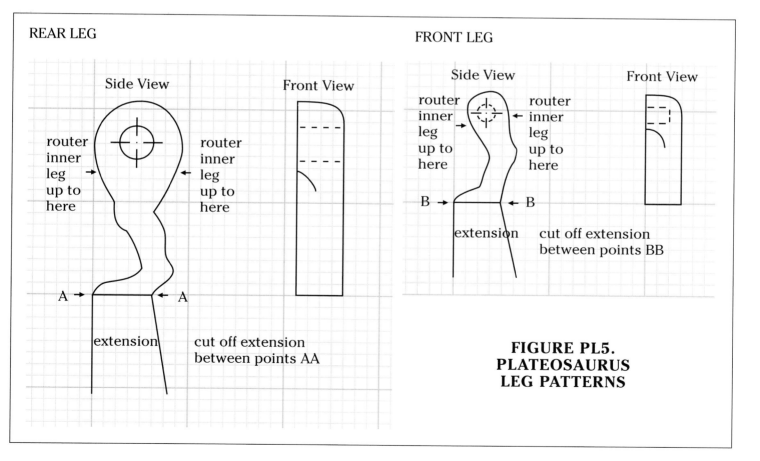

REAR LEG

Side View

Front View

router
inner
leg
up to
here

router
inner
leg
up to
here

A →   ← A

extension   cut off extension
between points AA

FRONT LEG

Side View

Front View

router
inner
leg
up to
here

router
inner
leg
up to
here

B →   ← B

extension   cut off extension
between points BB

**FIGURE PL5.
PLATEOSAURUS
LEG PATTERNS**

Stegosaurus armatus

Stegosaurus (STEG-uh-sawr-us): "Roofed lizard"
Order: Ornithischia
Suborder: Stegosauria
Family: Stegosauridae
Genus: *Stegosaurus*
Species: *Stegosaurus armatus*

Close relatives: *Stegosaurus ungulatus* and Diracodon
Length: Up to 30 feet (9.14 meters)
Height: Up to 11 feet (3.3 meters) at the hips
Weight: Up to 3 tons (2.7 metric tons)

Stegosaurus armatus, the largest of the Stegosaur family, is the only plated dinosaur known to have inhabited what is now North America. It was first discovered by the team of Benjamin Mudge and Arthur Lake while working for Othniel Marsh in 1877. These first remains were unearthed from the Late Jurassic Morrison Formation of Colorado. Additional skeletons have since been found in Wyoming, Utah, and Oklahoma.

Stegosaurus was primarily quadrupedal despite the fact that the rear legs were twice as long as the front. It has traditionally been held that in this position, this rather ungainly looking creature browsed for food on the ground as it ambled along at a speed significantly slower than other dinosaurs. A new theory, however, has emerged about Stegosaurus's stance. It is thought that the massive hind legs in association with the smaller front ones, a uniquely

constructed spine, and a tail acting as a counterbalance allowed the beast to rear up to a tripodal pose with the tail acting as a third support. Standing so, Stegosaurus could reach higher-growing plants.

The feet supporting Stegosaurus's bulk were comparatively small and narrow. On the front pair, there were five toes per foot, while in back, there were only four. All digits possessed hoof-like claws.

In relation to the rest of the body, the head was incredibly tiny. The small jaws had a sharp, horn-covered beak in front and weak teeth along the sides. These features are cited by some authorities as reasons why Stegosaurus could not have eaten anything other than very small amounts of soft food. Consequently, it is asserted the animal must have been cold-blooded. It is currently argued, however, that they may well have had gizzard stones aiding digestion. Such would allow the consumption of coarse foods in large quantities and would be indicative of a high metabolic rate.

One of the legendary features of Stegosaurus was its incredibly minuscule brain. It is generally described as being the size of a walnut or golf ball. Even more renowned was the "second brain" in the hips. In fact, there was a relatively large cavity in the hips to house a swelling of the spinal cord. This was not, however, a second brain. It was merely a large nerve ganglia that helped move and control the large hips and tail.

Probably the most discussed aspect of Stegosaurus is its most noticeable, the tall plates that ran along its back from neck to tail. Several theories exist as to their function. All have their supporters and detractors.

In fact, it is uncertain just how these plates, which could grow to 4 feet in height, were actually positioned. Some authorities maintain they were upright but debate whether they were in pairs or staggered. Other scientists believe the plates lay flat against the body. Because the plates were merely attached to the skin and not a part of an underlying skeleton, still other writers think it was possible for them to be raised and lowered at will between the vertical and horizontal.

One of the theories as to the purpose of the plates is that they were for attraction or identification between the sexes. The fact that both males and females seem to have had them weakens this idea, however. It is possible, though, that the young did not have these protrusions, and so they may have served to distinguish between juveniles and adults.

A more commonly held opinion is that the plates, which contained a complex network of blood vessels, were used as heat exchangers to regulate body temperature. In the sun, they acted as solar heaters. In the shade, they could be employed to dispense excess heat. If this is what the plates were for, a staggered arrangement makes more sense. Such would allow the breeze to circulate between them, and it would prevent their blocking one another from solar rays. Movability would have enhanced the plates' effectiveness as temperature-regulating devices. They could be readily positioned to absorb or dispense heat as needed.

Still, the most traditional and strongly supported belief is that the plates were for defense. For this purpose, they are routinely portrayed upright. As with so many other things, though, this positioning provokes controversy. It is said that as such, they really only served to protect the backbone, which really did not need such defense, because it was set very deep beneath tall, vertical spines. Those who believe the plates could be moved up and down can better argue their protective role. They show that when lowered, the plates could overlap and cover the otherwise vulnerable shoulders, flanks, and hips. Other scientists uphold that while of a defensive nature, the plates really served no function other than to increase the size of the animal to intimidate enemies.

The four long, paired, horn-covered spikes at the end of Stegosaurus's tail were undoubtedly used as defensive weapons. The powerful tail, lacking the stiffening rods of some other Ornithischians, was very flexible. Consequently, the spikes could be flailed about with lethal force.

All of this leads to the question of Stegosaurus's reaction when attacked. One authority wonders how the spikes could have been effective if they stood upright but the tail was swept from side to side. The protectiveness of the plates if rigidly vertical also presents problems to the same individual. This leads to his theory that when assaulted, Stegosaurus may have curled up in a ball on its side like a hedgehog. As such, it would have presented a circle of shielding plates in conjunction with a sweeping, spiked tail that kept predators at bay.

Another theory on the method of defense is more traditional in that the animal is thought to have stayed on its feet, but it holds that the beast moved differently than is generally supposed. In essence, Stegosaurus bounced on its short front legs so that it could pivot on its rear ones. This allowed it to react quickly to either face its opponent or present its tail for a deadly swipe. At the same time, the plates could be lowered to protect from above.

Stegosaurus young probably hatched from eggs. The remains of juveniles grown beyond the hatchling stage have been found. These reflect animals about the size of large dogs. There are indications that the young grew to adulthood in as little as six years. If this is the case, the Stegosaurus would have had a very high metabolic rate.

Stegosaurus lived along riverbanks and lakeshores, as well as farther upland. While it searched for food in these areas, it was always on its guard against predators like Allosaurus and Ceratosaurus.

BODY CONSTRUCTION
Step 1.
See Steps 1 to 3 for Camptosaurus. The Stegosaurus pattern is represented in fig. ST2. An alternative body plan, fig. ST3, is also offered if you wish to make the Stegosaurus with its tail held higher off the ground.
Step 2.
With a $3/8$-inch round-over bit, completely router both sides of the body.
Step 3.
With a $3/8$-inch brad-point bit, drill both leg holes at a 90-degree angle through the body.
Step 4.
With a $1/8$-inch brad-point bit, at a 90-degree angle to the side of the head, drill the eye holes to a depth of $1/16$ inch (see fig. ST4).

REQUIRED MATERIALS

Body: One $11^{1}/_{2}$ x $3^{1}/_{2}$ x $3/4$-inch piece of stock
Rear legs: Two 9 x 2 x $3/4$-inch pieces of stock
Front legs: Two 8 x $1^{1}/_{4}$ x $3/4$-inch pieces of stock
Plates: One 10 x 3 x $1/4$-inch piece of stock
Spikes: One 6-inch length of $3/16$-inch-diameter dowel rod
Other: Four $3/8$-inch-diameter axle pegs for the legs, and one 6-inch length of $1/8$-inch-diameter dowel rod for the plate pegs

Step 5.
With a $1/16$-inch bit, at a 45-degree angle to the side of the head, drill the nostril holes to a depth of $1/16$ inch (see fig. ST4).
Step 6.
Mark the four points on the top of the end of the tail for the holes for the spikes (see fig. ST5).

Step 7.
With a $3/16$-inch brad-point bit, at the designated angles, drill the four holes in the tail for the spikes to a depth of $1/8$ inch. *Do not exceed this depth.*
Step 8.
Mark and carve the mouth in accordance with the Type B method (see figs. ST2 and ST4).

Step 9.
Lay out the plate patterns (see fig. ST6) on the $1/4$-inch-thick piece of stock. A total of eighteen plates of various sizes are required.

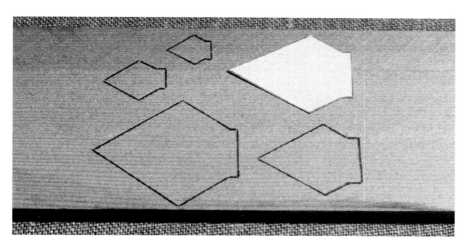

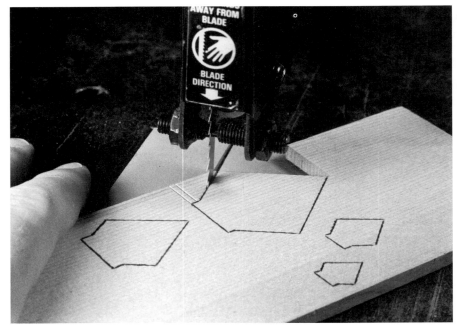

Step 10.
Using a band saw or scroll saw, cut out the plates.

Step 11.
Sand the bottoms of the plates to ensure they are perfectly flat and squared with the sides.

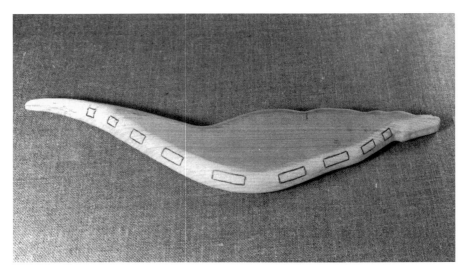

Step 12.
With a pencil, mark the sections along the two rounded edges of the back where the plates will go (see fig. ST7). The intent is to produce a series of staggered, short, chamfered areas alternating with rounded areas. Although the two lines of plates are to be staggered, it does not matter on which side the process begins or ends. Mark the length of each area to be chamfered to match exactly the actual length of the base of the particular plate that will be affixed at that point. The completed chamfers should be at roughly a 60-degree angle off a line perpendicular to the side of the body. In all cases, despite the size of the plate, the width of the area to be removed should not exceed $1/4$ inch.

Step 13.
With a modeling knife, cut crosswise and perpendicularly into the wood along the two lines delineating the ends of each plate chamfer. Execute to a depth at which the maximum length of the cut is $1/4$ inch.

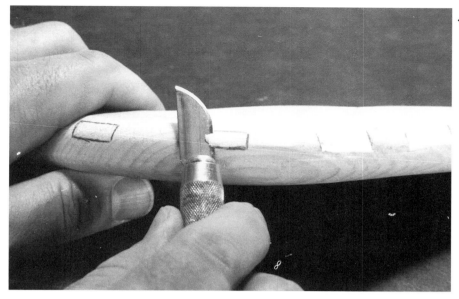

Step 14.

Using the same knife, carve out the undesired wood between each pair of cuts. Be careful to keep the overall depth constant in between.

Step 15.

If necessary, even up the surfaces of the chamfers. Rifflers are best for this task, if you have them. As indicated (see fig. ST8), the completed chamfers should uniformly be at a 60-degree with a line perpendicular to the side of the body.

Step 16.

Make certain each plate fits properly in its assigned location. Adjust the plate or chamfer as required by sanding, carving, or rasping.

Step 17.

Find the exact center point on the bottom of each plate and mark it with an awl.

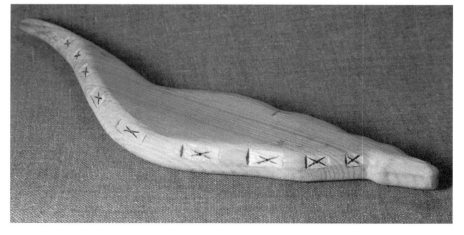

Step 18.

Find the center point on each chamfered area and mark it with an awl.

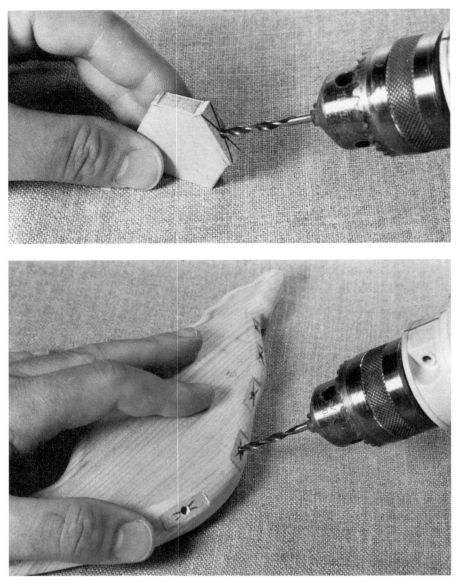

Step 19.
With a ⅛-inch brad-point bit, at a 90-degree angle to the bottom of each plate and the surface of each chamfer, drill a hole ⅛ inch deep at each of the points just marked.

Step 20.
Now use the modeling knife to cut eighteen ¼-inch-long pieces from the 6-inch length of ⅛-inch-diameter dowel rod.

Step 21.
Being careful not to get glue on the bottom surfaces of the plates that could later affect the fit, glue a peg into each hole and let dry.

Step 22.
From the 6-inch section of 3/16-inch-diameter dowel rod, cut four 1¼-inch lengths for the spikes.

Step 23.
By sanding, taper one end of each of the four dowel pieces to a rounded point, (see fig. ST5).

Step 24.
Sand the body, plates, and spikes to a fine finish.

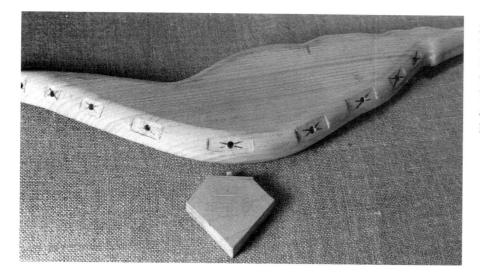

Step 25.
Place a drop of glue in each of the holes in the chamfered areas on the back, and affix the plates to the body, being careful to keep them aligned and at the proper angles. Let dry.

Step 26.
Place a drop of glue in each of the four holes for the spikes, and affix the spikes. Be careful to keep them aligned and at the proper angle (see fig. ST5). Let dry.

LEG CONSTRUCTION
Both the front and rear legs are made using the Type A construction method (see figs. ST9 and ST10).

Step 1.
Use a $^3/_8$-inch brad-point bit to drill the holes through all four legs for the axle pegs.

Step 2.
Router the designated areas on all four legs with a $^3/_8$-inch round-over bit.

Step 3.
Exclusive of the thickness of the heads, cut all four axle pegs to lengths of $1^1/_8$ inches.

FINISHING AND ASSEMBLY
Step 1.
Finish as desired.
Step 2.
Assemble as per basic Type A leg construction.

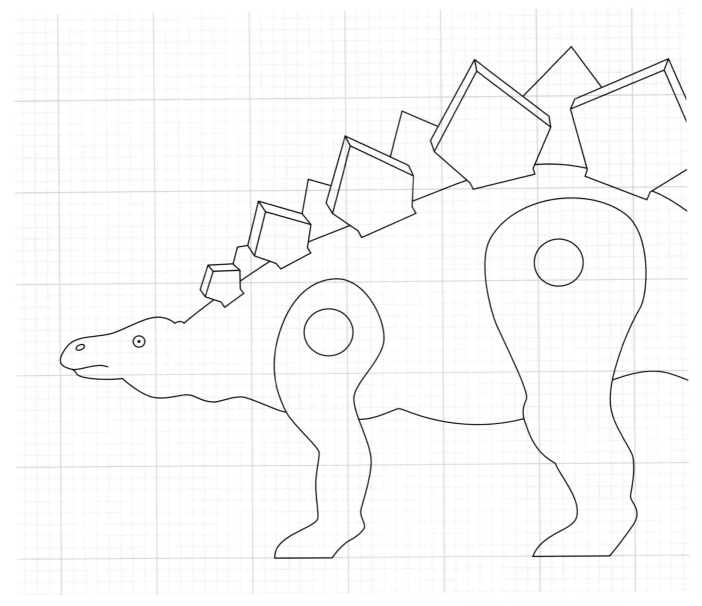

FIGURE ST1. PLAN OF COMPLETED STEGOSAURUS (FULL-SCALE)

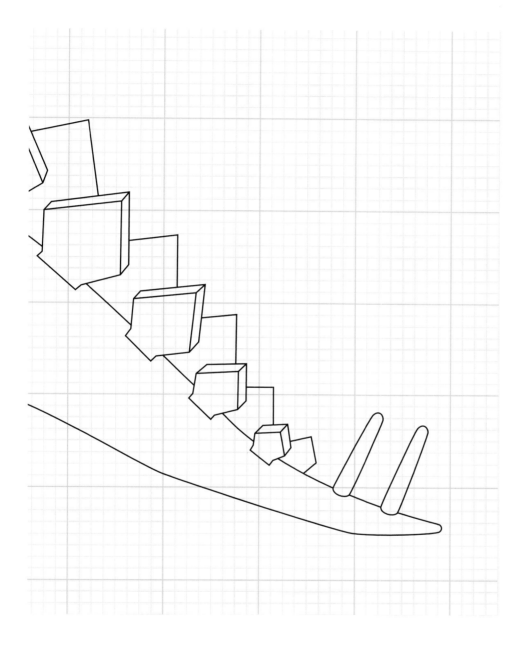

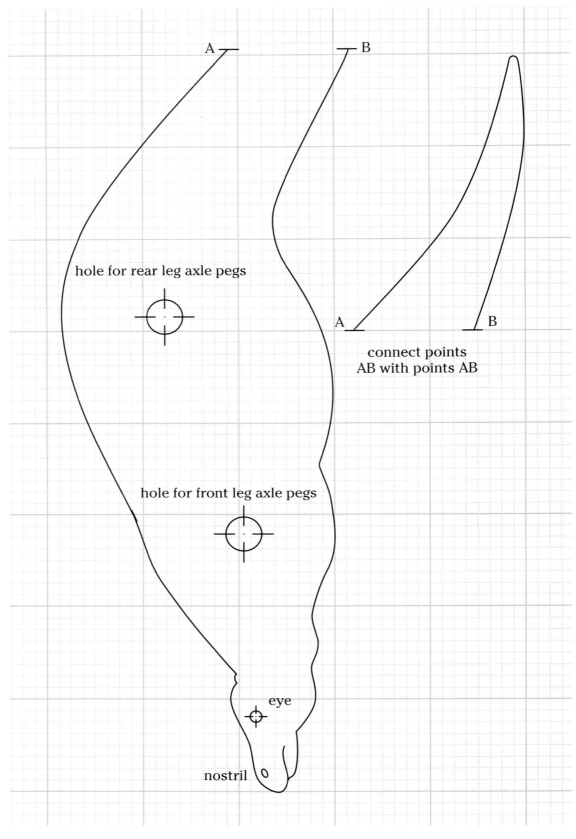

FIGURE ST2. BODY PATTERN FOR STEGOSAURUS

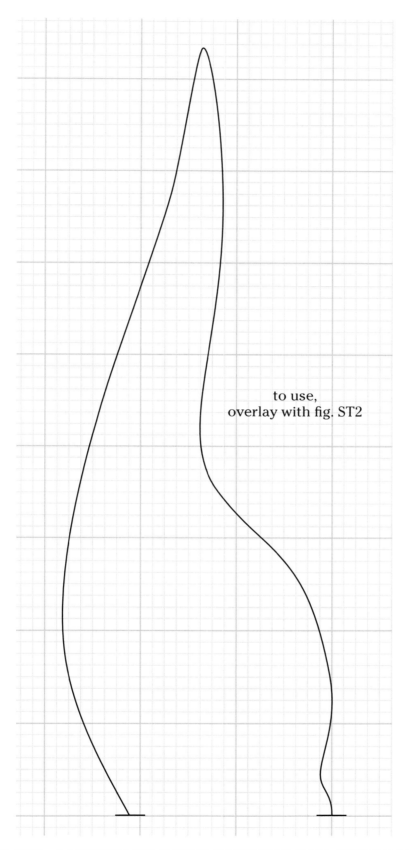

to use,
overlay with fig. ST2

FIGURE ST3. ALTERNATE BODY PATTERN FOR STEGOSAURUS

POSITIONS AND ANGLES
OF EYES AND NOSTRILS

SPIKE POSITIONS AND ANGLES
CROSS-SECTIONED AT POINTS AA

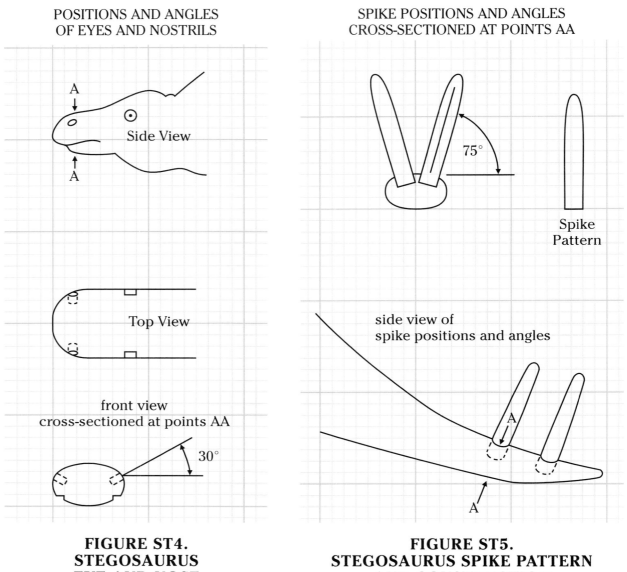

Side View

Top View

front view
cross-sectioned at points AA

30°

75°

Spike
Pattern

side view of
spike positions and angles

**FIGURE ST4.
STEGOSAURUS
EYE AND NOSE
CONSTRUCTION**

**FIGURE ST5.
STEGOSAURUS SPIKE PATTERN
AND CONSTRUCTION**

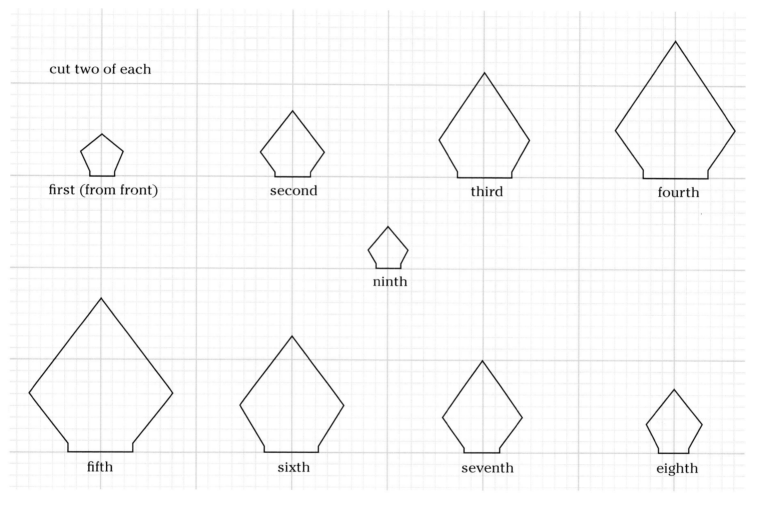

cut two of each

first (from front) second third fourth

ninth

fifth sixth seventh eighth

FIGURE ST6. STEGOSAURUS PLATE PATTERNS

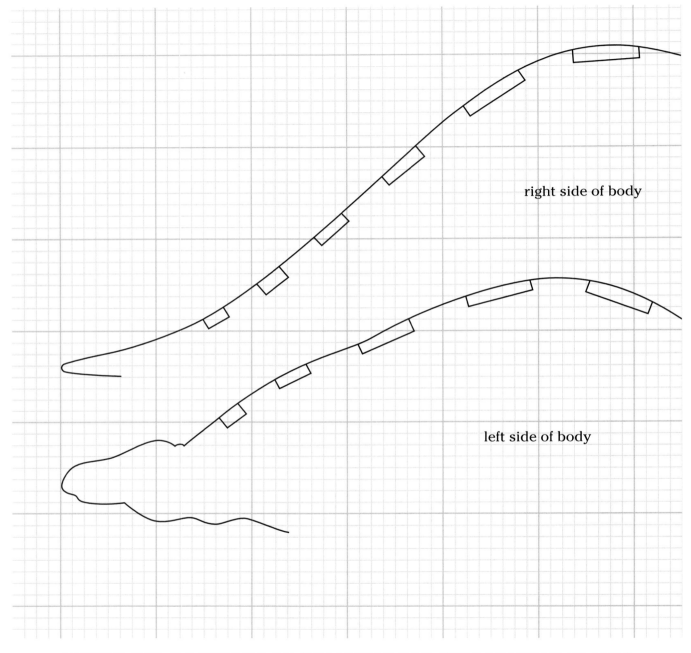

right side of body

left side of body

FIGURE ST7. POSITIONS OF CHAMFERS FOR STEGOSAURUS PLATES

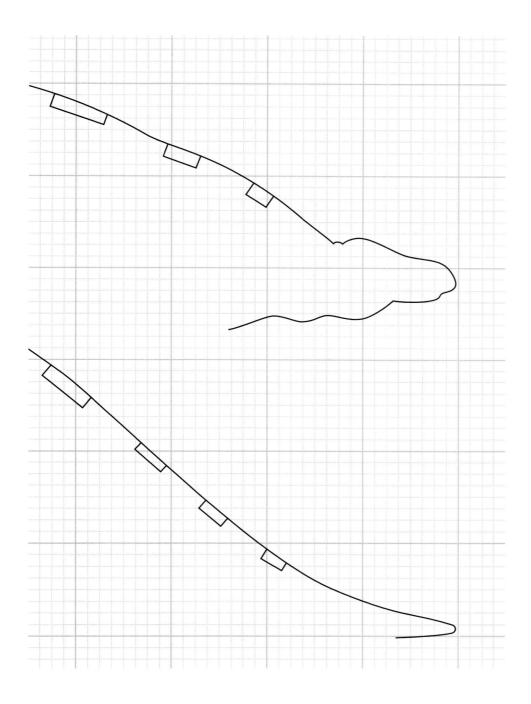

PLATE WITH DOWEL PEG IN PLACE

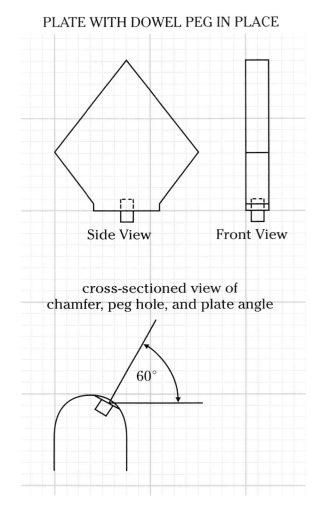

Side View   Front View

cross-sectioned view of
chamfer, peg hole, and plate angle

60°

FIGURE ST8. STEGOSAURUS PLATE CONSTRUCTION

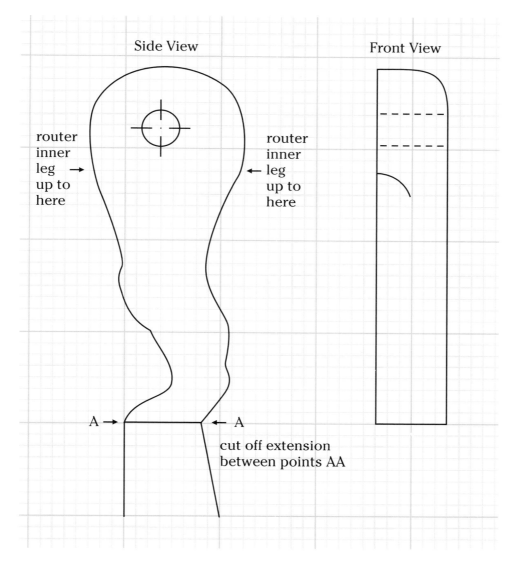

Side View

Front View

router
inner
leg →
up to
here

router
inner
← leg
up to
here

A → ← A

cut off extension
between points AA

FIGURE ST9. STEGOSAURUS REAR LEG PATTERN

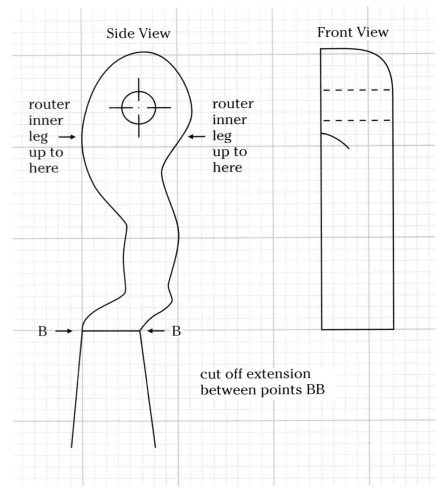

FIGURE ST10. STEGOSAURUS FRONT LEG PATTERN

PREHISTORIC PLANT PROJECTS

Pleuromeia

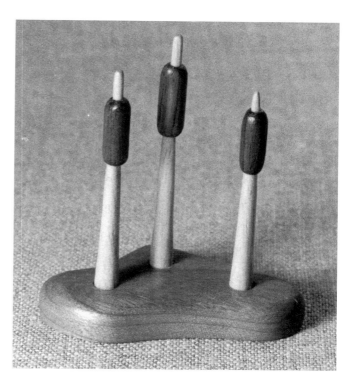

Pleuromeia was a plant that evolved during the predinosaur Carboniferous period and survived through the Permian and into the Triassic. These tall, slender plants were vascular in nature, which means they possessed roots, stems, and leaves, and they functioned through photosynthesis like modern vegetation. There were, however, no flowering plants at that time, and like ferns today, pleuromeia reproduced through spores rather than seeds or pollen. A relative of the club mosses and horsetails that still exist, pleuromeia grew in swampy terrain. It shared the landscape during the Triassic period with palmlike cycads and early conifers.

BASE CONSTRUCTION

Step 1.
Lay out the base pattern (see fig. PLR2) on the designated piece of stock. Leave enough wood extending from one end for a 4-inch handle.

Step 2.
Mark the three points for the holes for the plant stems.

Step 3.
Being sure to leave an extension for a handle, use a band saw to cut out the base.

REQUIRED MATERIALS

Base: One $2^3/4$ x $1^1/2$ x $3/8$-inch piece of stock with enough extra wood for a 4-inch extension off one end

Plant stalks: One $5^1/2$-inch length of $1/4$-inch-diameter dowel rod

Plant tips: One $1^1/2$-inch length $1/8$-inch-diameter dowel rod

Plant flowers: One $2^1/2$-inch length of $1/4$-inch-diameter dowel rod

Note: If a natural finish is desired, use different types of wood for the base and various parts of the plant. If a variety of woods cannot be used, stain the different sections contrasting hues.

Step 4.
With a $1/4$-inch round-over bit, router around the top edge of the base.

Step 5.
Now cut off the extension, and router the remaining portion of the edge.

Step 6.
With a $1/4$-inch brad-point bit, at a 90-degree angle to the surface of the base, drill the three holes that will receive the dowel stems.

Step 7.
Sand the base to a fine finish.

Step 8.
Finish the base as desired and put aside.

PLANT CONSTRUCTION
Step 1.
From the $5^1/2$-inch section of $1/4$-inch-diameter dowel rod, cut three pieces, $1^{13}/_{16}$ inches, $1^7/_8$ inches, and 2 inches in length.

Step 2.
By sanding, taper all but $3/8$ inch of the length of each dowel piece to a $1/8$-inch-diameter end to create the plant stalks (see fig. PLR3).

Step 3.
From the $2^1/2$-inch section of $1/4$-inch dowel rod, cut three pieces, one $11/_{16}$ inch and two $3/4$ inch in length.

Step 4.
Use a small center finder to locate the center points at each end of these three short dowel pieces, and mark them with an awl.

Step 5.

With a ¹⁄₈-inch brad-point bit, drill a hole ¹⁄₈ inch deep directly into one end of each of the three short dowel sections at the point marked.

Step 6.

With a ³⁄₃₂-inch bit, drill a hole ¹⁄₈ inch deep directly into the opposite end of each short dowel piece at the point marked.

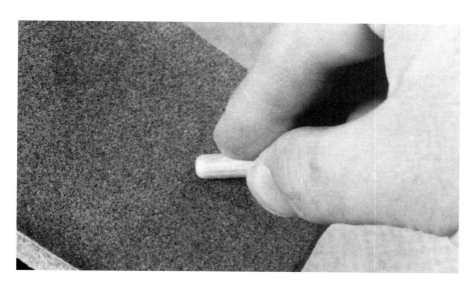

Step 7.

By sanding, round off the edges at both ends of each short dowel section to create the plant tops (see fig. PLR3).

Step 8.

From the length of ¹⁄₈-inch-diameter dowel rod, by sanding, reduce the diameter of ¹⁄₂ inch of length to ³⁄₃₂ inch, taper the end to ¹⁄₁₆ inch in diameter, and round off the tip (see plant tips in fig. PLR3).

Step 9.
With a modeling knife, cut off the ½-inch length just fashioned.
Step 10.
Following the same procedure, make two more pieces, ³/₈ inch and ⁷/₁₆ inch long.
Step 11.
Fine-sand all of the pieces.

FINISHING AND ASSEMBLY
Step 1.
If contrasting woods were not used for the various parts, stain them as desired and allow to dry.

Step 2.
To assemble the plant, put the short stalk pieces with the short top ones, the midlength stalk pieces with the midlength ones, and the longer stalk pieces with the longer ones (see figs. PLR1 and PLR3).
Step 3.
Glue the plant top pieces to the appropriate plant stalk pieces, align, and let dry.
Step 4.
Then glue the plant tip pieces to the appropriate plant top pieces, align, and let dry.

Step 5.
Finish with varnish or oil.
Step 6.
Glue the three plants into the holes in the base, being careful to keep the stalks perpendicular with the base and parallel with each other.

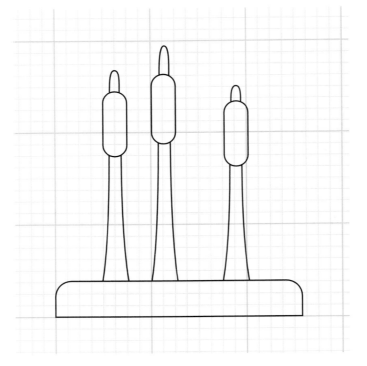

FIGURE PLR1. PLAN OF COMPLETED PLEUROMEIA PLANT (FULL-SCALE)

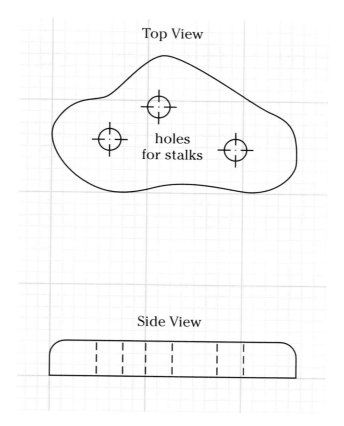

Top View

holes
for stalks

Side View

FIGURE PLR2. PLEUROMEIA BASE PATTERN

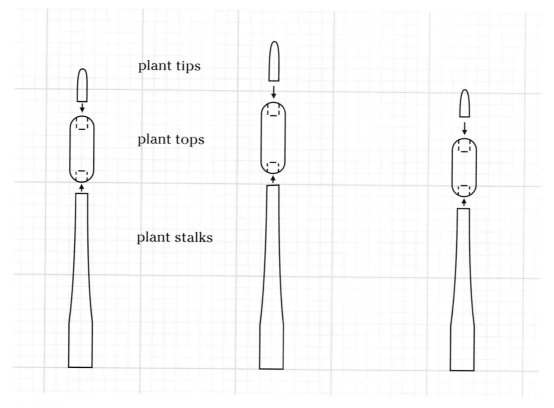

plant tips

plant tops

plant stalks

FIGURE PLR 3. PLEUROMEIA PLANT PATTERNS AND ASSEMBLY

Fern

Ferns also first evolved during the Carboniferous period. Lasting through all three eras of the Age of Dinosaurs, many forms are still seen today. Generally preferring a humid environment, some of the early forms could grow to the size of large trees. The fronds issued from separate stalks and produced spores for reproduction.

REQUIRED MATERIALS

Base: One 2¹/₂ x 1¹/₂ x ¹/₂-inch piece of stock, with enough extra wood for a 4-inch extension off one end

Stalks: One 15-inch length of ¹/₈-inch-diameter dowel rod

Fronds: Box of round toothpicks

CONSTRUCTING THE BASE

Step 1.
Lay out the base pattern (fig. F2) on the designated piece of stock, leaving enough wood extending from one end for a 4-inch handle.

Step 2.
Mark the six points for the holes for the plant stems.

Step 3.
With the band saw, cut out the base and handle extension.

Step 4.
Router the upper edge of the base with a ¹/₄-inch round-over bit.

Step 5.
Now cut off the handle extension, and router the remaining part of the edge.

Step 6.
Starting with the two centermost holes and at the angles indicated (see fig. F2), use a $1/8$-inch brad-point bit to drill the six holes for the dowel stalks. The outer four holes will cut into the center ones. This is OK.

Step 7.
Sand to a fine finish and put aside.

PLANT CONSTRUCTION

Step 1.
The 15-inch length of $^1/_8$-inch-diameter dowel rod from which the stalk pieces will be cut needs to be steamed into a gentle curve. To do so, first fill a 12-inch-diameter pan with water and bring to a fast boil.

Step 2.
Lay the dowel across the pan for one hour, working it gently every ten minutes to help soften it up and enhance the bow.

Step 3.
Take a piece of scrap wood at least 15 inches long and $2^1/_2$ inches wide, and drive in some finishing nails in the pattern shown in the photograph.

Step 4.
When the dowel becomes soft, bend it around the center nail and hook the dowel ends behind the nails at either end. Let dry.

Step 5.
With a modeling knife, cut the following lengths from the bent $^1/_8$-inch-diameter dowel rod:
> One $2^7/_{16}$-inch length
> Two $2^3/_8$-inch lengths
> Two $2^3/_{16}$-inch lengths
> One $1^{15}/_{16}$-inch length

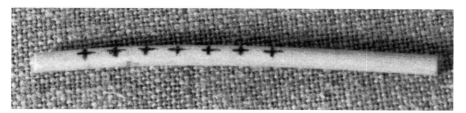

Step 6.
On the $2^7/_{16}$-inch piece and one of the $2^3/_8$-inch lengths, starting 1 inch up from what will be the bottom end, use a pencil to mark a point every $^3/_{16}$ inch along one side (see fig. F3). Flip the dowel over, and beginning at a spot $1^3/_{32}$ inch from the bottom end, mark a point every $^3/_{16}$ inch. This second row should be staggered with those on the opposite side. Repeat the process with the three longest of the remaining stalks, but start $^3/_4$ inch up. Do the same with the shortest piece, beginning $^5/_8$ inch up.

Fern • 169

Step 7.

At what will be the tip end of each dowel stalk, find the center point and mark with an awl.

Step 8.

Place one stem piece in a small clamp or vise that will allow it to lie flat and keep it from turning. This will help maintain the alignment of the holes when drilling.

Step 9.

Now, down the centerline of the upper side of the dowel, re-mark the points at $^{3}/_{16}$-inch intervals with an awl. Be careful not to apply too much pressure to avoid splitting the dowel.

Step 10.

With a $^{3}/_{64}$-inch bit, drill a hole halfway through the dowel at every point marked, except the one closest to the end. All holes, other than the one near the end, should be at a 90-degree angle to the length of the dowel. The hole near the end should project toward the tip at a 45-degree angle (see fig. F3).

Step 11.

Repeat the procedure for the remaining stalk pieces, then reverse each stalk piece and repeat on the opposite side.

Step 12.

On each stalk piece, toward the tip, on the side with the last hole farthest from the tip, mark a point halfway between that hole and the tip.

Step 13.

With a $^{3}/_{64}$-inch bit, at a 45-degree angle toward the tip, drill holes at these new points to a depth of $^{1}/_{16}$ inch.

Step 14.

With the same bit, drill a hole directly into the end of each dowel stalk at the marked center point. These holes should be $^{3}/_{32}$ inch deep.

Step 15.

By sanding, round the tip of each stalk.

Step 16.

From the round toothpicks, you will need to cut twelve $^{1}/_{4}$-inch lengths, twelve $^{5}/_{16}$-inch lengths, and seventy-eight $^{3}/_{8}$-inch lengths for the fronds. First, working in from both ends of each toothpick, find the points where the diameter increases to $^{1}/_{16}$ inch and mark. With a modeling knife, cut off both tips at these points.

Step 17.

Now, from the new ends, mark in $^{1}/_{4}$, $^{5}/_{16}$, or $^{3}/_{8}$ inch, depending on the size you are making, and mark. With the modeling knife, cut off the ends at the new marks.

Step 18.

By sanding, round off the thicker end of each piece.

Step 19.

Fine-sand all dowel and toothpick pieces.

Step 20.

Now assemble each frond (see fig. F3). The two bottommost holes on each stalk receive $^{1}/_{4}$-inch-long leaves. The next two holes each get $^{5}/_{16}$-inch leaves. All the other holes have $^{3}/_{8}$-inch leaves affixed in them. Place a small amount of glue into each hole, and wedge a dowel leaf of appropriate size into each hole. Be sure all leaves along the sides are aligned with each other and those at the end angle are at 45 degrees toward the tip.

FINISHING AND ASSEMBLY

Step 1.

Finish the base and fronds as desired.

Step 2.

Glue the fronds to the base. The two with leaves starting 1 inch up go in the center holes. Arrange the other fronds around them as desired.

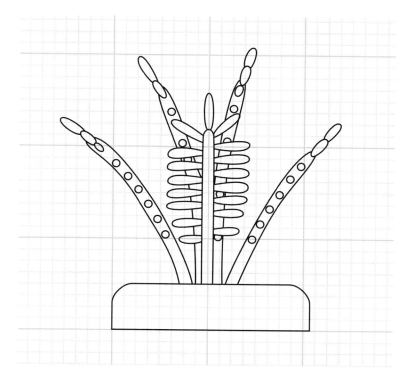

FIGURE F1. PLAN OF COMPLETED FERN (FULL-SCALE)

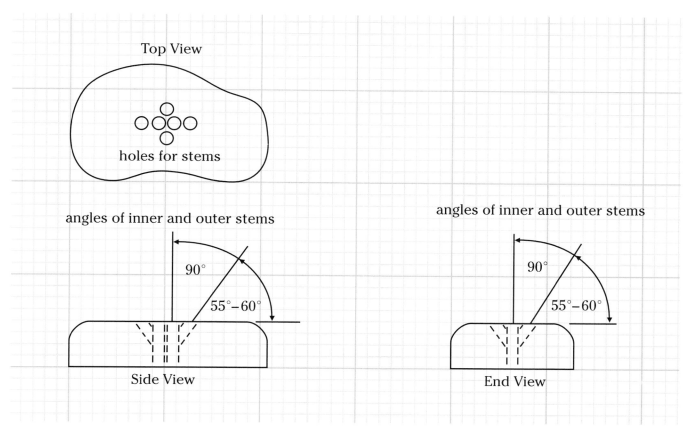

Top View

holes for stems

angles of inner and outer stems

90°

55°–60°

Side View

angles of inner and outer stems

90°

55°–60°

End View

FIGURE F2. FERN BASE PATTERN AND CONSTRUCTION

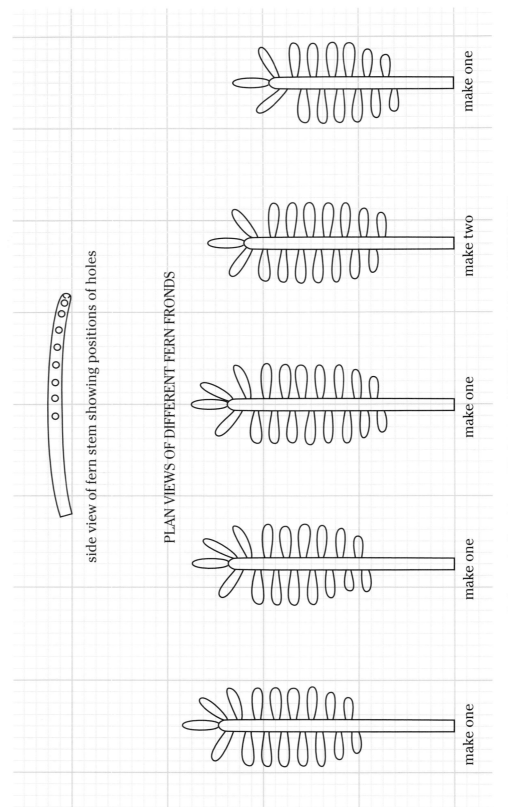

side view of fern stem showing positions of holes

PLAN VIEWS OF DIFFERENT FERN FRONDS

make one

make two

make one

make one

make one

FIGURE F3. FERN FROND PATTERNS AND ASSEMBLY

Palm Trees

Palm trees evolved during the Cretaceous period. Like much of the other vegetation that came into being at that time, palms were true flowering plants. They produced pollen and seeds, which were spread around by various creatures feeding on them. The tough, fibrous fronds, and even the trunks, were eaten by a number of herbivorous Cretaceous dinosaurs described in this book. Palms shared the landscape with other modern tree types such as oaks and hickories.

BASE CONSTRUCTION

Step 1.

Lay out the base pattern (see fig. PT1) on the designated piece of stock. Mark the center points for the holes that will accommodate the tree trunks.

Step 2.

Use a band saw to cut out the base.

Step 3.

With a ³/₄-inch brad-point or Forstner bit, drill the two holes for the tree trunks at the angles designated (see fig. PT1). It is intended that the second hole cut into and overlap the first.

REQUIRED MATERIALS

Base: One 6 x 5 x ³/₄-inch piece of stock

Tree trunks: One 15 x 2 ¹/₂ x ³/₄-inch piece of stock

Tree top centers: One 8-inch length of 1¹/₈-inch-diameter dowel rod

Fronds: One 14-inch length of 2 x 4 and one 6-inch length of 1³/₄ x ³/₄-inch stock

Other: One 12-inch length of ¹/₈-inch-diameter dowel rod and several round toothpicks for use as pegs

Note: If a natural finish is desired, use different types of wood for the base and various sections of the tree. If a variety of woods cannot be used, stain the different sections contrasting hues.

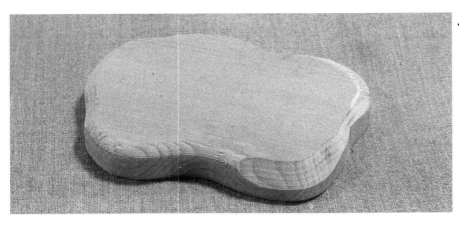

Step 4.
To create a somewhat varied edge to the base, use a ³/₄-inch chamfer and a ³/₈-inch round-over bit to router different sections of what will be the upper edge.

Step 5.
Now use a belt sander to shape and vary the configuration of the routered areas even more.

TREE TRUNK CONSTRUCTION
Step 1.
Lay out the two tree trunk patterns (see fig. PT2) on the designated piece of stock. At one end of each, leave an additional 4 inches for a handle to hold when routering.

Step 2.
Use a band saw to cut out the tree trunks.

Step 3.
With a ³/₈-inch round-over bit, completely router all four edges of each tree trunk piece.

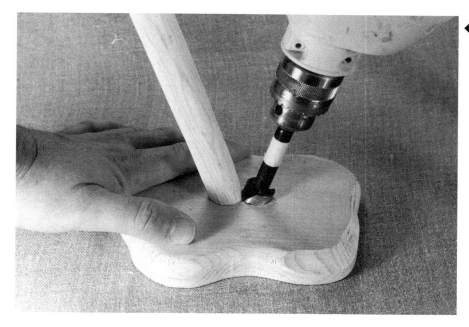

▶ Step 4.

Insert and align the larger tree trunk piece in its proper hole. With it in place, redrill the second hole using a $^3/_4$-inch bit.

Step 5.

From the $1^1/_8$-inch-diameter dowel rod, cut two pieces 4 inches long.

Step 6.

Find the center points at each end of each dowel section and make a shallow mark with an awl.

Step 7.

With a $^1/_4$-inch round-over bit, router all around the marked end of each dowel piece.

Step 8.

Mark each piece $1^1/_8$ inches up from the routered end, and use the band saw to cut off the excess length.

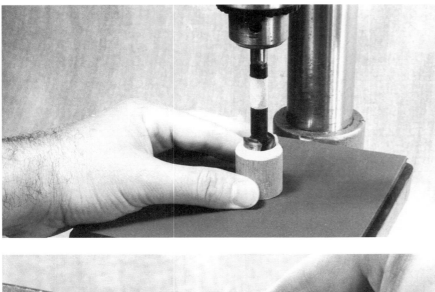

Step 9.
With a ³/₄-inch brad-point or Forstner bit, at the center point of the routered end, drill a hole ¹/₂ inch deep straight into each dowel piece (see fig. PT3).

◀ **Step 10.**
With a belt sander or by carving, shape the unroutered end of each dowel section to a rounded point (see fig. PT3).

Step 11.
At this point, without gluing, check the fit of the trunks to the base and the tops to the trunks. If pieces do not fit, adjust as necessary by opening up the holes a little or removing a small amount of wood from the ends of the trunk pieces.

FROND CONSTRUCTION
Step 1.
From the 2 x 4, cut two sections 3³/₄ inches long.
Step 2.
On the 4-inch side of the two 2 x 4 sections, lay out a series of ten large frond profile patterns (see figs. PT4 and PT5). Lay out the patterns so the ten are layered and will nest with each other. Reverse the pattern, alternating thick and thin ends. Allow some waste material at the top and bottom.

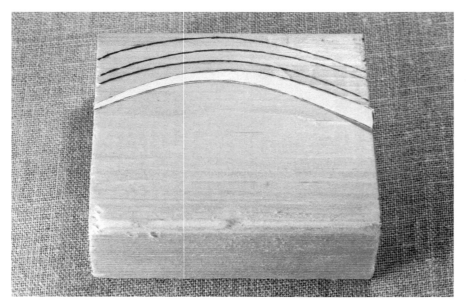

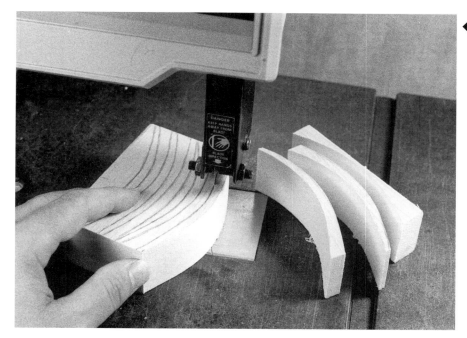

◀ **Step 3.**
With the band saw, cut out the ten pieces from each 2 x 4 section. Be careful to note and maintain the sequence in which they were cut.

Step 4.
Inclusive of the top and bottom waste, restack the pieces in the order they were cut. Align the edges and wrap tightly with a thin layer of masking tape.

Step 5.
With the wrapped 2 x 4 sections set on their long edges, lay out the top view pattern for the large fronds (see figs. PT5 and PT6).

Step 6.
Now use the band saw to cut out the leaves from top to bottom. Be careful when completing the final cut, because the tape will be severed. This will probably produce somewhat rough pieces of slightly varying size. This is OK.

Step 7.
With a belt sander, shape the edge of each frond to create a nice, uniform, elliptical form.

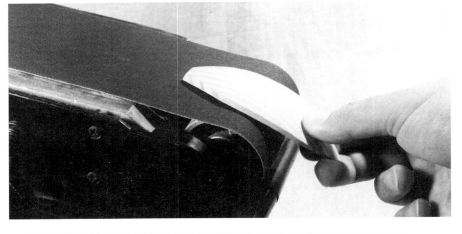

Next, sand the top and bottom of each frond to an even smoothness.

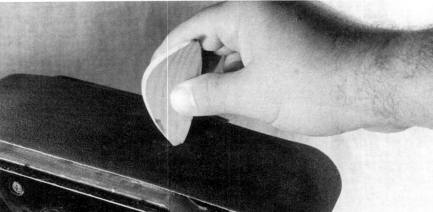

Finally, sand the thick end flat, creating a small rectangular surface, roughly $5/16$ inch top to bottom, and $3/16$ inch wide. The plane of this surface should be perpendicular to the top line of the frond at that end (see figs. PT7 and PT8).

Step 8.

On the top of each frond, mark an evenly spaced series of V notches along each edge (see fig. PT7).

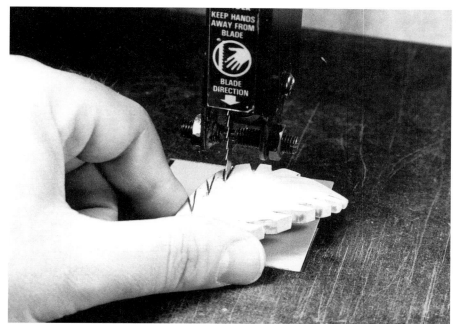

◀ **Step 9.**

Now use the band saw to cut the notches in each leaf. Because the frond pieces will be resting on only two points during cutting, be very careful not to let them wobble from side to side.

Step 10.

From the remaining length of 2 x 4, cut two pieces that are $2^7/_8$ inches long. These are for the larger of the medium-size fronds, and each block will also produce ten parts. Follow the same procedure as for the large fronds.

Step 11.

From the 6 x $1^3/_4$ x $^3/_4$-inch section of stock, cut two pieces that are $1^5/_8$ inches long and two pieces that are $1^1/_4$ inches long. The larger sections will produce five of the smaller medium-size fronds. The other two will each make five of the smallest. Follow the same procedure as for the larger fronds.

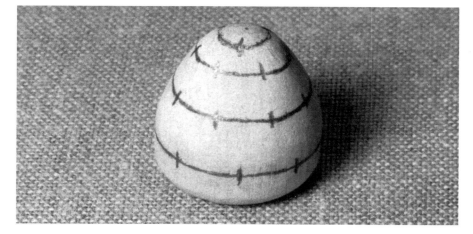

Step 12.

Next, on the tree top center piece, mark a line all around the circumference $^3/_8$ inch up from the bottom. Then, $^{13}/_{32}$ inch above this, mark a second line all around. A third line around should be marked $^{11}/_{32}$ inch above the second. Distances between lines are calculated on the surface of the tree top center, not on a perpendicular line. Finally, mark a fourth line $^9/_{32}$ inch above the third.

Step 13.
Along the bottom line, mark eight equally spaced points. In essence, divide the circumference into eighths.

Step 14.
Repeat the procedure on the second line, staggering the eight points with those on the first line.

Step 15.
Around the third line, mark six points that are evenly spaced but unaligned with those below.

Step 16.
On the fourth line of one top, mark three points that are evenly spaced with each other and staggered with the six on the third line.

Step 17.
On the fourth line of the other top, mark only two points. These should be opposite each other and unaligned with those below.

Step 18.
For each level, note which spots on the center piece will receive which fronds. There is no designated order for varying frond sizes in a given line. Arrange them in a manner that pleases you.

Step 19.
To fit the fronds around the tree top center piece (see fig. PT10), first set out the tree top center, and around it, lay out six of the large fronds and two of the medium-large. If the fit is too tight for all eight fronds to meet at the center, reduce their width by sanding a little off the edges.

Step 20.
For the second line of the center piece, do the same as with the first, but use two large fronds, five medium-large, and one small-medium.

Step 21.
On the third line, do the same again, using four small-medium and two small on one, and three small-medium and three small on the other.

Step 22.
Check each frond's angle of projection with the squared, thick, flat end against the center piece at its appropriate point of attachment. All fronds in a given circle should basically present the same angle. If not, adjust by sanding the face of the squared end.

Step 23.
Find the center point of the flattened end on each frond and mark it with an awl.

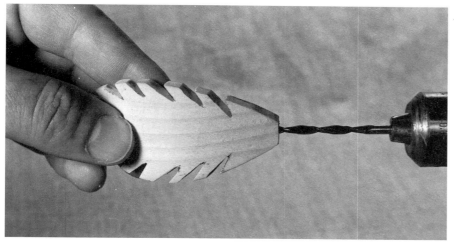

◀ Step 24.
With a ¹/₈-inch brad-point bit, at a 90-degree angle to the flattened surface, drill a hole ¹/₄ inch deep into the end of each large, medium-large, and small-medium frond (see fig. PT8).

Step 25.
Follow the same procedure for the small fronds, using a ¹/₁₆-inch bit.

◀ Step 26.
By sanding, decrease the width (from side to side) of the rectangular ends of the fronds. In essence, taper the frond ends even more, bringing the vertical edges of each rectangle closer to the edge of each hole.

Step 27.
Without gluing, fit the tree top center pieces over the tree trunks. With a pencil, make a mark denoting the alignment of the two pieces with each other.

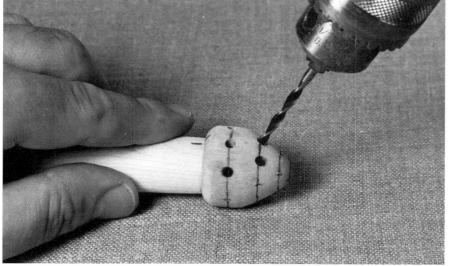

◀ Step 28.
On the treetop center pieces, at those points designated to receive the three larger sizes of fronds, use a ¹/₈-inch brad-point bit, at a 90-degree angle to the surface at each particular point, to drill a hole ¹/₄ inch deep (see fig. PT9).

Step 29.
Follow the same procedure at those points designated to receive the small fronds, using a ¹/₁₆-inch drill bit.

FINISHING AND ASSEMBLY

Step 1.
Sand all parts to a fine finish, being careful not to eradicate the alignment marks for tops and trunks.

Step 2.
If parts are to be stained, do so at this time, and allow to dry.

Step 3.
Now glue the trunk pieces to the base.

Step 4.
Finish the trunk and base section, the tree top centers, and the fronds as desired.

Step 5.
From the 20-inch length of $1/8$-inch-diameter dowel rod, with a modeling knife, cut forty $1/2$-inch lengths.

Step 6.
From round toothpicks, at the points where the diameter is $1/16$ inch, cut ten to twelve $1/2$-inch lengths.

Step 7.
Glue the $1/8$-inch-diameter pegs into the holes in the three larger sizes of fronds, and the $1/16$-inch-diameter pegs into the holes in the smallest size. Let dry.

Step 8.
Working quickly, align the tree top centers on the trunks and glue in place. Before the tops dry, glue the fronds in their proper places around them. Adjust the angles and let dry.

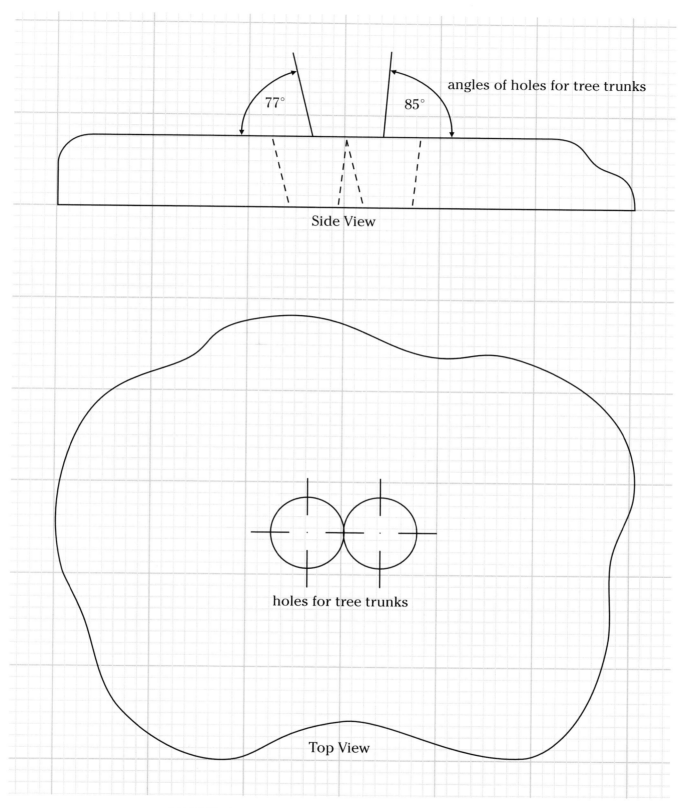

angles of holes for tree trunks

77° 85°

Side View

holes for tree trunks

Top View

FIGURE PT1. PALM TREE BASE PATTERN

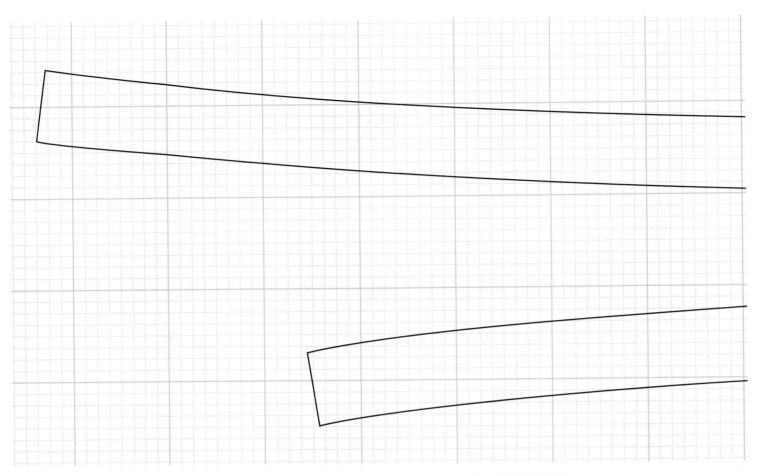

FIGURE PT2. PALM TREE TRUNK PATTERNS

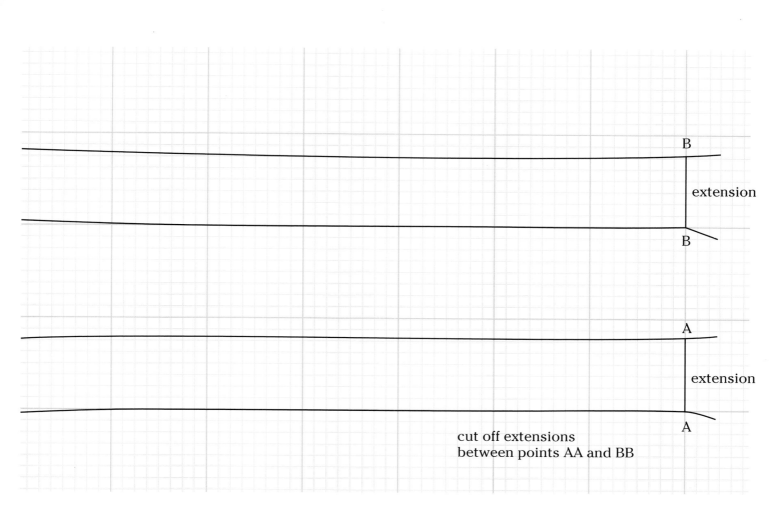

B

extension

B

A

extension

cut off extensions
between points AA and BB

A

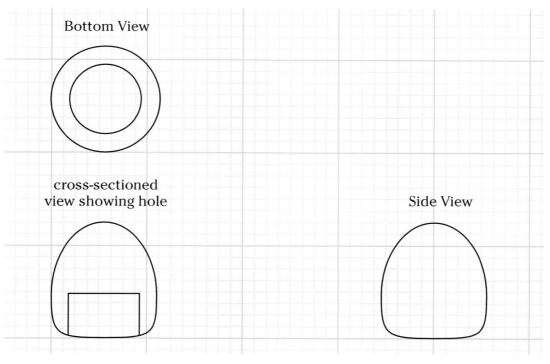

Bottom View

cross-sectioned
view showing hole

Side View

FIGURE PT3. PATTERN FOR PALM TREE TOP CENTERS

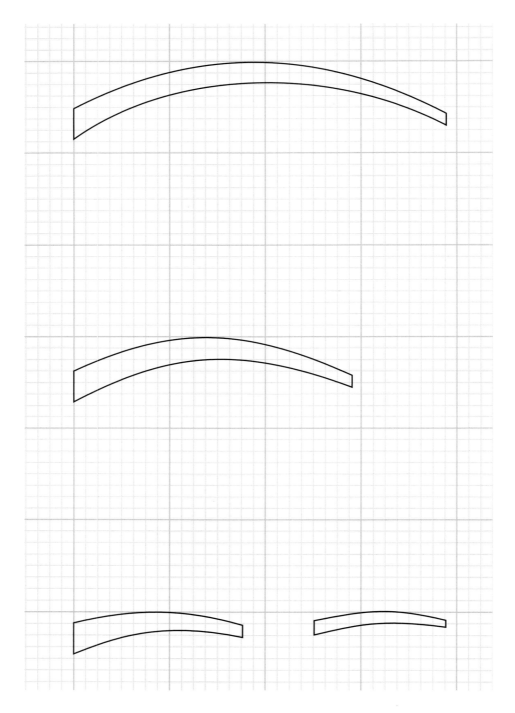

FIGURE PT4. PROFILE PATTERNS OF PALM TREE FRONDS

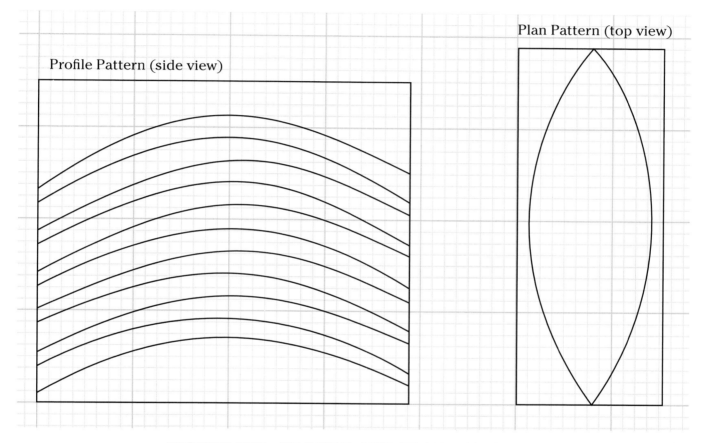

Profile Pattern (side view)

Plan Pattern (top view)

**FIGURE PT5. PROFILE AND PLAN PATTERNS
OF PALM TREE FRONDS LAID OUT ON 2 X 4 STOCK**

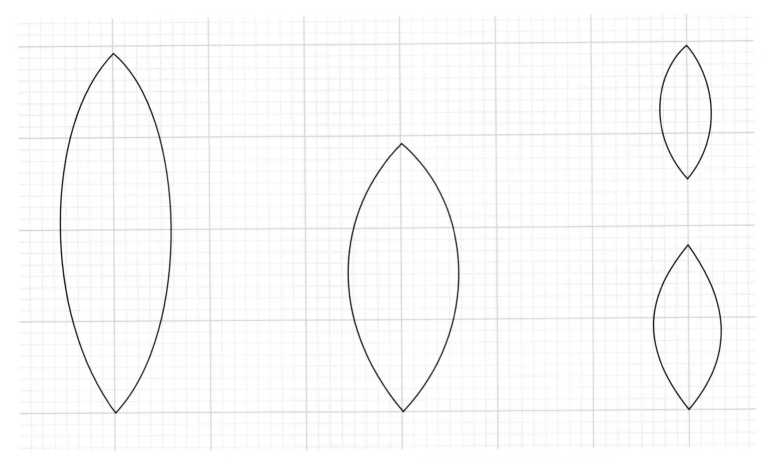

FIGURE PT6. PLAN PATTERNS OF PALM TREE FRONDS

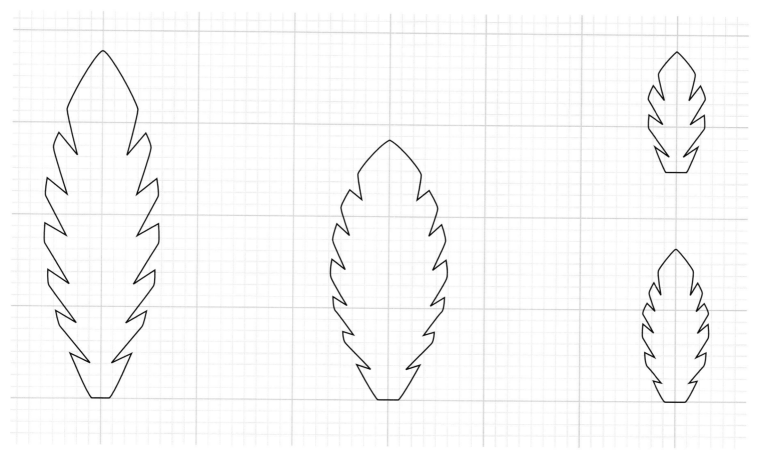

FIGURE PT7. PLAN PATTERNS FOR NOTCHING PALM TREE FRONDS

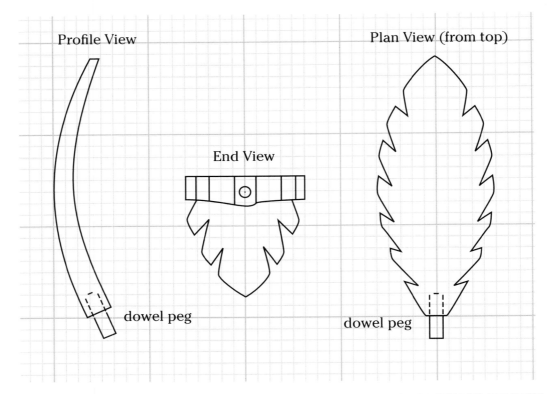

Profile View

Plan View (from top)

End View

dowel peg

dowel peg

FIGURE PT8. THREE VIEWS OF COMPLETED PALM TREE FROND

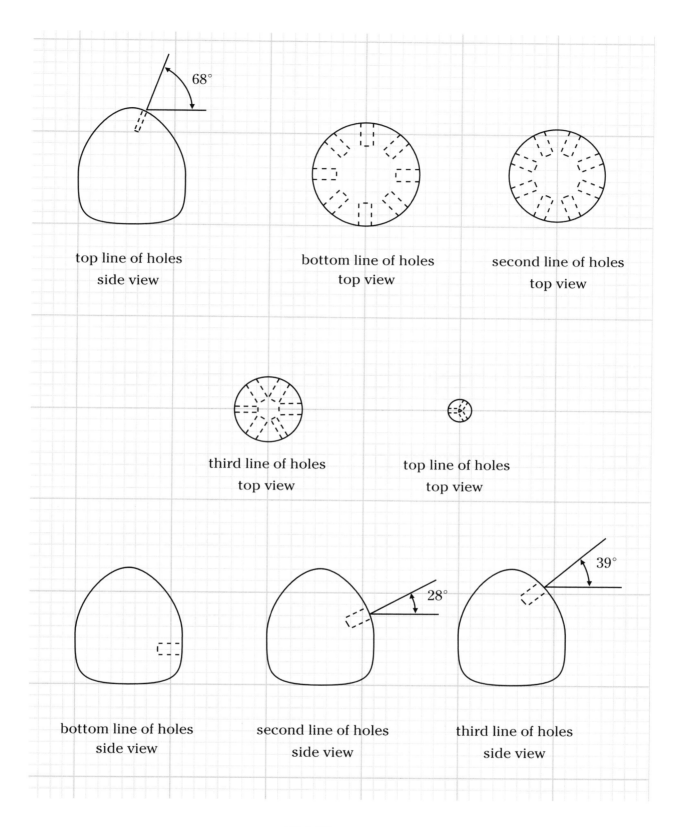

top line of holes
side view

bottom line of holes
top view

second line of holes
top view

third line of holes
top view

top line of holes
top view

bottom line of holes
side view

second line of holes
side view

third line of holes
side view

FIGURE PT9.
POSITIONS AND ANGLES OF HOLES FOR PEGS IN PALM TREE TOP CENTERS

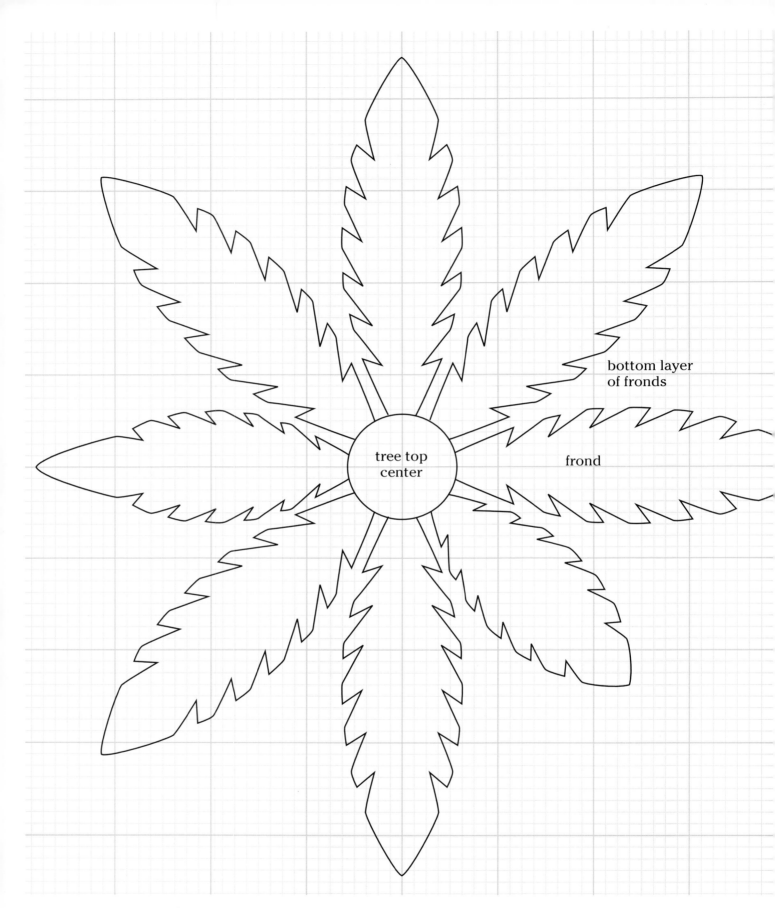

tree top
center

bottom layer
of fronds

frond

**FIGURE PT10. EXAMPLE PLAN VIEW OF
FRONDS ASSEMBLED WITH PALM TREE TOP CENTER**

Bibliography

Alexander, R. McNeill. *Dynamics of Dinosaurs and Other Extinct Giants*. New York: Columbia University Press, 1989.

Bakker, Robert T. *The Dinosaur Heresies: New Theories Unlocking the Mystery of the Dinosaurs and Their Extinction*. New York: William Morrow and Company, 1986.

Case, Gerard R. *A Pictorial Guide to Fossils*. New York: Van Nostrand Reinhold Company, 1982.

Charig, Alan. *A New Look at the Dinosaurs*. New York: Facts on File, 1979, 1983.

Colbert, Edwin H. *A Fossil-Hunter's Notebook: My Life with Dinosaurs and Other Friends*. New York: E. P. Dutton, 1980.

————. *The Great Dinosaur Hunters and Their Discoveries*. New York: Dover Publications, 1968, 1984.

Czerkes, Sylvia J., and Everett C. Olson, eds. *Dinosaurs Past and Present*. 2 Vols. Introduction by John M. Harris. Seattle: Natural History Museum of Los Angeles County in association with the University of Washington Press, 1987.

Desmond, Adrian J. *The Hot-Blooded Dinosaurs: A Revolution in Paleontology*. New York: The Dial Press/James Wade, 1976.

The Diagram Group. *A Field Guide to Dinosaurs: The First Complete Guide to Every Dinosaur Now Known*. New York: Avon Books, 1983.

Fortey, Richard. *Fossils, the Key to the Past*. New York: Van Nostrand Reinhold Company, 1982.

Gaffney, Eugene S. *Dinosaurs*. Illustrated by John D. Dawson. New York: Golden Press, 1991.

Gillette, David D., *Seismosaurus: The Earth Shaker*. Illustrated by Mark Hallett. New York: Columbia University Press, 1993, 1994.

Gillette, David D., and Martin G. Lockley, eds. *Dinosaur Tracks and Traces*. Cambridge: Cambridge University Press, 1989.

Glut, Donald F. *The Dinosaur Dictionary*. Introductions by Alfred Sherwood Romer and David Techter. Secaucus, NJ: The Citadel Press, 1972.

Halstead, L. B. *The Search for the Past: Fossils, Rocks, Tracks and Trails: The Search for the Origin of Life*. Garden City, NY: Doubleday & Company Inc. 1982.

Halstead, L. B. and Jenny Halstead. *Dinosaurs*. Poole, Dorset: Blandford Press, 1981.

Horner, John R., and Don Lessem. *The Complete T. Rex*. New York and London: Simon and Schuster, 1993.

Horner, John R., and James Gorman. *Digging Dinosaurs: The Search that Unraveled the Mystery of Baby Dinosaurs*. Foreword by David Attenborough. Illustrated by Donna Braginetz and Kris Ellingsen. New York: Workman Publishing, 1988.

Kricher, John C. *Peterson First Guide to Dinosaurs*. Illustrated by Gordon Morrison. Boston: Houghton Mifflin Company, 1990.

Kricher, John, and Gordon Morrison. *A Field Guide to Dinosaurs Coloring Book*. Boston: Houghton Mifflin Company, 1989.

Lambert, David. *The Ultimate Dinosaur Book*. Foreword by John H. Ostram. New York: Dorling Kindersley in association with The Natural History Museum, London, 1993.

The Last of the Dinosaurs. San Francisco: Bellerophon Books, 1978.

Long, Robert A., and Samuel P. Welles. *All New Dinosaurs and Their Friends from the Great Recent Discoveries*. San Francisco: Bellerophon Books, 1975.

McGowan, Christopher. *Dinosaurs, Spitfires, and Sea Dragons*. Cambridge, MA: Harvard University Press, 1983, 1991.

McLoughlin, John C. *Archosauria: A New Look at the Old Dinosaur*. New York: The Viking Press, 1979.

Norman, David. *Dinosaur!* New York: Prentice Hall, 1991.

Paul, Gregory S. *Predatory Dinosaurs of the World: A Complete Illustrated Guide*. New York: Simon and Schuster, 1988.

Psihoyos, Louis. *Hunting Dinosaurs*. With John Knoebber. New York: Random House, 1994.

Ratkevich, Ronald Paul. *Dinosaurs of the Southwest*.

Illustrated by John C. McLoughlin. Albuquerque, NM: University of New Mexico Press, 1976.

Russell, Dale A. *An Odyssey in Time: The Dinosaurs of North America*. Minocqua, WI: North Word Press in association with the National Museum of Natural Sciences, Canada, 1989.

Sattler, Helen Roney. *Dinosaurs of North America*. Illustrated by Anthony Rao. Introduction by John H. Ostram. New York: Lothrop, Lee & Shepard Books, 1981.

———. *The Illustrated Dinosaur Dictionary*. Foreword by John H. Ostram. Illustrated by Pam Carroll. New York: Lothrop, Lee & Shepard Books, 1983.

Steel, Rodney, and Anthony Harvey, eds. *The Encyclopedia of Prehistoric Life*. Foreword by W. E. Swinton. New York: McGraw-Hill Book Company, 1979.

Stewart, Ron. *Dinosaurs of the West*. Missal, MT: Mountain Press Publishing Co., 1988.

Stout, William. *The Dinosaurs: A Fantastic View of a Lost Era*. Edited by Byron Press. Narrated by William Service. Introduction and scientific commentary by Peter Dodson. New York: Bantam Books, 1981.

Wilford, John Noble. *The Riddle of the Dinosaur*. New York: Alfred A. Knopf, 1985.

Zallinger, Peter. *Dinosaurs and Other Archosaurs*. Foreword by John H. Ostram. New York: Random House, 1986.

Metric Conversions

INCHES TO MILLIMETERS

IN.	MM	IN.	MM
1	25.4	51	1295.4
2	50.8	52	1320.8
3	76.2	53	1346.2
4	101.6	54	1371.6
5	127.0	55	1397.0
6	152.4	56	1422.4
7	177.8	57	1447.8
8	203.2	58	1473.2
9	228.6	59	1498.6
10	254.0	60	1524.0
11	279.4	61	1549.4
12	304.8	62	1574.8
13	330.2	63	1600.2
14	355.6	64	1625.6
15	381.0	65	1651.0
16	406.4	66	1676.4
17	431.8	67	1701.8
18	457.2	68	1727.2
19	482.6	69	1752.6
20	508.0	70	1778.0
21	533.4	71	1803.4
22	558.8	72	1828.8
23	584.2	73	1854.2
24	609.6	74	1879.6
25	635.0	75	1905.0
26	660.4	76	1930.4
27	685.8	77	1955.8
28	711.2	78	1981.2
29	736.6	79	2006.6
30	762.0	80	2032.0
31	787.4	81	2057.4
32	812.8	82	2082.8
33	838.2	83	2108.2
34	863.6	84	2133.6
35	889.0	85	2159.0
36	914.4	86	2184.4
37	939.8	87	2209.8
38	965.2	88	2235.2
39	990.6	89	2260.6
40	1016.0	90	2286.0
41	1041.4	91	2311.4
42	1066.8	92	2336.8
43	1092.2	93	2362.2
44	1117.6	94	2387.6
45	1143.0	95	2413.0
46	1168.4	96	2438.4
47	1193.8	97	2463.8
48	1219.2	98	2489.2
49	1244.6	99	2514.6
50	1270.0	100	2540.0

The above table is exact on the basis: 1 in. = 25.4 mm

U.S. TO METRIC

1 inch	=	2.540 centimeters
1 foot	=	.305 meter
1 yard	=	.914 meter
1 mile	=	1.609 kilometers

METRIC TO U.S.

1 millimeter	=	.039 inch
1 centimeter	=	.394 inch
1 meter	=	3.281 feet or 1.094 yards
1 kilometer	=	.621 mile

INCH-METRIC EQUIVALENTS

Fraction	Decimal Equivalent Customary (IN.)	Metric (MM)	Fraction	Decimal Equivalent Customary (IN.)	Metric (MM)
1/64	.015	0.3969	33/64	.515	13.0969
1/32	.031	0.7938	17/32	.531	13.4938
3/64	.046	1.1906	35/64	.546	13.8906
1/16	.062	1.5875	9/16	.562	14.2875
5/64	.078	1.9844	37/64	.578	14.6844
3/32	.093	2.3813	19/32	.593	15.0813
7/64	.109	2.7781	39/64	.609	15.4781
1/8	.125	3.1750	5/8	.625	15.8750
9/64	.140	3.5719	41/64	.640	16.2719
5/32	.156	3.9688	21/32	.656	16.6688
11/64	.171	4.3656	43/64	.671	17.0656
3/16	.187	4.7625	11/16	.687	17.4625
13/64	.203	5.1594	45/64	.703	17.8594
7/32	.218	5.5563	23/32	.718	18.2563
15/64	.234	5.9531	47/64	.734	18.6531
1/4	.250	6.3500	3/4	.750	19.0500
17/64	.265	6.7469	49/64	.765	19.4469
9/32	.281	7.1438	25/32	.781	19.8438
19/64	.296	7.5406	51/64	.796	20.2406
5/16	.312	7.9375	13/16	.812	20.6375
21/64	.328	8.3384	53/64	.828	21.0344
11/32	.343	8.7313	27/32	.843	21.4313
23/64	.359	9.1281	55/64	.859	21.8281
3/8	.375	9.5250	7/8	.875	22.2250
25/64	.390	9.9219	57/64	.890	22.6219
13/32	.406	10.3188	29/32	.906	23.0188
27/64	.421	10.7156	59/64	.921	23.4156
7/16	.437	11.1125	15/16	.937	23.8125
29/64	.453	11.5094	61/64	.953	24.2094
15/32	.468	11.9063	31/32	.968	24.6063
31/64	.484	12.3031	63/64	.984	25.0031
1/2	.500	12.7000	1	1.000	25.4000